A SHARED DESTINY

A SHARED DESTINY

Near East Regional Development and Cooperation

edited by

Joyce R. Starr

with the assistance of

Addeane S. Caelleigh

1983

Published in cooperation with
**THE CENTER FOR
STRATEGIC AND INTERNATIONAL STUDIES**
Georgetown University

PRAEGER SPECIAL STUDIES • PRAEGER SCIENTIFIC

Library of Congress Cataloging in Publication Data
Main entry under title:

A Shared destiny.

"Published in cooperation with the Center for Strategic and International Studies, Georgetown University."
Includes index.
Contents: Introduction / Joyce Starr — The European contribution / Max Kohnstamm — The Marshall Plan revisited / Nadeem Maasry — [etc.]
1. Near East—Economic policy—Addresses, essays, lectures. I. Starr, Joyce. II. Caelleigh, Addeane S. III. Georgetown University. Center for Strategic and International Studies.
HC415.15.S52   1983   338.956   83-9709
ISBN 0-03-063757-0

Published in 1983 by Praeger Publishers
CBS Educational and Professional Publishing
a Division of CBS Inc.
521 Fifth Avenue, New York, New York 10175 U.S.A.

©1983 by The Center for Strategic and International Studies

3456789   041   987654321

Printed in the United States of America

CONTENTS

LIST OF TABLES

FOREWORD

David M. Abshire

The impact of economic development on prospects for global and regional peace has been repeatedly demonstrated throughout the twentieth century. Some feel that if Lord Keynes's advice to forgive World War I war debts had been adopted, the devastating postwar inflation and depression that undermined peace in Europe might have been avoided. Later, the generosity and hard-headed economic sense embodied in the Marshall Plan helped to restore a war-torn Europe.

Today in the troubled Middle East, economic development is vital for providing the necessary foundation on which to build a lasting peace. The possibility that constructuve steps might be taken to encourage Near East neighbors—Egypt, Israel, Jordan, and Lebanon—to further their own economic development by cooperative ventures must be fully explored. A major challenge we now confront is conceiving creative mechanisms by which the private and public sectors of Europe, the United States, and the countries of the Near East can work together economically to strengthen their fragile relations.

I am proud that the Center for Strategic and International Studies (CSIS) has made a major effort in this regard. The work of Joyce R. Starr, CSIS overseas representative in the Near East, demonstrates that a private, scholarly organization like CSIS can assist in furthering such efforts through practical recommendations that can be taken up by the parties most concerned. Starr's work over the past four years, through the Near East Development Forum, has been instrumental in initiating significant programs to encourage Near East economic projects that benefit individual nations, regional interaction, and the prospects for peace in the region.

Under her direction and under CSIS auspices, cabinet-level delegations from Egyptian and Israeli governments have met with senior government officials and financiers from the United States and Europe, to examine the prospects for expanding Egyptian-Israeli trade and economic cooperation. The participants' common desire has been to strengthen the Egyptian-Israeli relationship through economic ties that would enable the two countries to weather the political storms inevitably on the horizon. The fact that bilateral economic relations have continued, despite the tensions resulting from Israel's move into Lebanon in the summer of 1982, is an encouraging sign that the basic promise of peace through economic cooperation is worth pursuing. Starr's current responsibility as director of the secretariat for the U.S. Business Commission on the Reconstruction of Lebanon, a body of U. S. corporate leaders examining opportunities and incentives for U.S. private-sector involvement in Lebanese reconstruction, has deepened our center's involvement in this important work.

The concept for this book grew initially from the Washington and Paris meetings of the Near East Development Forum in 1981. Since that time, the scope of discussions has been broadened to include many of the issues raised in this book. One of the key elements of our center's success has been its ability to serve as a catalyst or "neutral agent," bringing together technical experts, political leaders, and financial supporters to examine common interests from a variety of viewpoints. No better example of this process could be found than the ideas reflected in A Shared Destiny.

David M. Abshire
President

Center for Strategic and
 International Studies
Georgetown University

x

ACKNOWLEDGMENTS

The history behind this book dates back to 1979, revolves around the energetic vision and persistence of several leading characters, with decisive moments and high drama against a backdrop of three continents. While that particular story will not be recounted in these pages, my warmest appreciation must be extended to the many who gave so generously of their time and confidence, including Ambassador Arthur Burns, Ambassador David Abshire, and noted economist Robert Nathan, whose wise counsel provided the necessary direction; Aaron Gafney, former Governor of the Bank of Israel, whose ideas gave shape to the process; and Abdel Razik Abdul Meguid, former Deputy Prime Minister of Egypt for Economic and Financial Affairs under Presidents Sadat and Mubarak, whose enthusiasm for the principles of peace inspired us to persevere. I am also indebted to the Ford Foundation and to the Edmond de Rothschild Foundation for their support of the CSIS Near East Development Forum from which this book evolved.

Finally, I wish to express my gratitude to colleagues: Catherine Maimon, for adept abilities in bringing plans to life; Addeane Caelleigh, for skillful and untiring editorial assistance; Marty Kalin, for analytical talents and writer's perseverance essential to the challenge of a manuscript; and Lela Palmer, for a job well done.

A SHARED DESTINY

1

INTRODUCTION: STRATEGIES FOR THE FUTURE

JOYCE R. STARR

John F. Kennedy wrote that "no problem of human destiny is beyond human beings. Man's reason and spirit have often solved the impossible and we believe they can do it again."

In the Near East, no issue is more intractable or seemingly insolvable than the question of peace. Even the very word, which took on almost mystical dimensions on that memorable November evening in 1979 when Anwar Sadat landed in Jerusalem, seems to have lost currency in the intervening years. The Lebanon War of 1982 was a stark reminder that a cessation of hostilities, in this case across the southern Lebanese border, could hold neither hope nor resemblance to peace. A further, and perhaps unanticipated, consequence of the armed confrontation between the Palestine Liberation Organization and Israel in the summer of 1982 was that the untried treaty between Israel and Egypt, not yet strengthened or reinforced through normal relations, quickly dissolved into what Egypt's Minister of State for Foreign Affairs B. Boutros Ghali calls the cold peace.

Regardless of the view one takes of the 1982 war and the negotiations that followed, changes have taken place in the region that provide both opportunity and incentive for political dialogue, particularly with reference to a freely negotiated settlement of the West Bank and the Gaza Strip. The overwhelming symbolic as well as physical importance of control over these territories and the mechanism by which transfers or adjustments in power and control take place cannot be overestimated. Our authors are fully aware of the importance and the sensitivity of these issues, although they do not address them directly. Rather, the challenge they address in A Shared Destiny is of a different order. This volume is premised on the view that the United States and its Western allies cannot rely exclusively on the political process to forge or to sustain peace between Israel and its Arab neighbors in the Near East. Traditional diplomatic approaches to resolving this conflict, however essential, should be augmented by strategies that simultaneously address the issues of regional development, interdependence, and cooperation. In spite of our ardor for the language of peace, so widely brandished to the point of abuse, the achievement of integrated relations among the countries of the Near East demands that we call upon an entirely new vocabulary of imagination and confidence.

Directing themselves to this task, our authors outline their thoughts on a variety of economic strategies and mechanisms that the West could employ to improve the prospects for regional cooperation and stability. None suggests that economic incentives alone can bring the warring states of the Near East to the negotiating table and thereby to peace and harmony. All recognize that the most fundamental requirement for resolution of the conflict is a genuine desire for peace on the part of the peoples and governments of the region. Even then, the search for accommodation will be frustrating, difficult, and lengthy, for the hostilities and fears of almost forty years of war will not be easily overcome. The authors nevertheless anticipate that the economic and material benefits of cooperative regional development will help bolster a fragile peace in its early stages and will strengthen bonds between those societies committing themselves to this process.

A Shared Destiny focuses on the relations between existing nation-states in the Near East and does not attempt to duplicate earlier in-depth analyses on the future of the West Bank and the Gaza Strip. Comprehensive research on the economics of a peace settlement were undertaken by an interagency task force of the U.S. government during the Carter administration.[1] One study indicates that increased cooperation between the West Bank and Gaza and the rest of the Arab world, particularly Jordan, as a result of a peace agreement or accommodation, could bring about a number of changes, including a gradual reduction in workers from these territories employed in Israel and a decline in the relative importance of Israel and the territories as trading partners. Overall, however, the authors hold the belief that trade, economic links, development programs, and other mutually beneficial aspects of an overall Middle East peace settlement will do more to ensure the ongoing success of long-term stability than any other factor. [2]

The chapter by Max Kohnstamm, former president of the European University Institute and one of the founders of the European Economic Community (EEC), underscores the importance of such interrelationships. Recalling the synergism through which Jean Monnet's vision for a peaceful, economically integrated Europe became reality, Kohnstamm suggests that the world might not have experienced World War II had there been in the 1920s or 1930s even a facsimile of the formalized contacts now existing only among the governors of Europe's central banks, much less the full range of cooperative institutions binding Europe today.

Looking at the crucial role of the U.S.-sponsored Marshall Plan in revitalizing the economies of war-torn Europe, Nadeem Maasry relates the lessons of that success to the exigencies of the Near East, specifically the necessities of external capital and managerial and technical assistance. The effectiveness of such outside assistance would be ensured by entrepreneurial initiative from within the region once cooperative ventures were under way.

Despite the dramatic results of the Marshall Plan in laying the foundations for the later establishment of the European Economic Communities, it is noteworthy that neither the United States nor the leading countries of Western Europe have made significant reference to this experience in devising their approach to settlement of the Arab-Israeli dispute. To the contrary, Western diplomatic initiatives appear to be based on the assumption that encouragement of cooperative relations between Israel and any of the Arab countries, specifically Egypt or Lebanon, will reduce the pressure on Israel to negotiate a solution to the West Bank dilemma, thus undermining Western interests in the region. Even at the time of the signing of the Camp David Agreement on March 26, 1979, little diplomatic attention was paid to the opportunities for economic interaction between Egypt and Israel. Despite the fact that voluminous research had been commissioned by the Carter administration on such prospects, the subject was not raised in the formal context of the negotiation proceedings.

While many will argue that any effort on the part of the West to enhance Israeli-Egyptian or Israeli-Lebanese relations will inversely affect Palestinian leverage, the reverse hypothesis could also be valid: that is, expanded ties between Israel and its neighbors would reduce Israel's sense of isolation, thereby increasing feelings of acceptance and security on the part of the Israeli people—which, in turn, could increase their confidence in, and desire for, an overall peace settlement. As Addeane Caelleigh points out in her examination of the potential for international conflict over water resources, short of major Western guarantees for an equitable resolution of the crippling 30-year water dispute between Jordan and Israel, Israel has no incentives—but some debilitating costs—in relinquishing the water resources of the West Bank and the Golan Heights. One might ask whether we might now see more rather than less progress in the autonomy negotiations if the United States had been prepared to commit its prestige and resources to Egyptian-Israeli economic cooperation to the extent that it promoted the political rapprochement in the Camp David talks.

In 1979 Congress took an important step in legislating a $5 million fund for cooperative projects "between Israel and her Arab neighbors," a sum that has since been reauthorized. In the first several years following the signing of the treaty, the major part of this fund remained in reserve owing to lack of suitable projects. While certainly not discouraging prospective applicants, the U.S. government took a narrow view in availing itself of this resource as a diplomatic option. Nonetheless, implicit in the establishment of the fund, irrespective of size, was the recognition that the United States has a responsibility to further cooperation and that additional resources are required to provide the necessary incentive to the parties involved.

The authors in this book subscribe to the thesis that regional cooperation strategies will not be effective unless they are compatible with the unique environment and circumstances of the Near East, supported by adequate resources and implemented through vehicles or mechanisms designed for this purpose.

Some will claim that mechanisms already exist to meet the development requirements of the Middle East. Addressing this question, Shireen Hunter discusses whether a Near East development fund would duplicate the responsibilities of existing banks and funds in the region. In her extensive survey of Middle East development institutions, Hunter concludes that room exists for at least one more development mechanism, which would specifically serve the interests of the Near East and not be hampered by the boycott requirement of existing funds in the area.

Robert Nathan and Jerome Levinson discuss the concept, need, and rationale for the establishment of a Near East development institution. Emphasizing the opportunity costs forgone by allocations of vast resources to military objectives, they argue that a more dramatic strategy is essential to ensure regional progress and peaceful coexistence. It is in this context that they propose the creation of a Near East peace and reconstruction fund, which would require substantial financial participation by the governments of the United

States and Western Europe and which would also facilitate private
sector involvement.

Fawzi Habib agrees with the need for an infusion of new resources to advance Near East development and integrative planning
but questions whether a new development institution is the most practical vehicle to accomplish these objectives, given the span of years
and extraordinary diplomatic commitment required to bring the concept to fruition—as juxtaposed on the urgent nature of the region's
economic problems. Habib recommends, instead, that the consortium approach to development financing, which has worked so effectively for individual countries (particularly in Latin America and Africa), be instituted for projects in the Near East affecting the interests of two or more nations. Under the consortium umbrella, the
process could begin whenever Western nations declared themselves
favorable to the task.

Nadeem Maasry concurs with Nathan and Levinson that only innovative strategies reinforced by an institutionalized mechanism will
succeed in capturing both the imagination of the Near East peoples
and their spirit of coexistence. He differs only in emphasizing reli-
ance on private, rather than public, financing.

Direct governmental sponsorship has both advantages and dis-
advantages. On the one hand, Western governments could be tempted
to use the newly created institution for political purposes that transcend its immediate charter. On the other, they could be instrumental in harmonizing tariff rates, reducing red tape, and ensuring the
successful implementation of the projects.

The Tel Aviv University Project for Joint Economic Development in the Middle East has completed extensive feasibility research
on 25 projects suitable for joint cooperation between Israel and Egypt.
Zeev Hirsch, who launched this effort, describes a number of areas
of potential cooperative benefit. Of the three components required
to produce fertilizer, for example, Egypt has nitrogen and phosphates,
while Israel can offer phosphates and potassium. A combination of
their resources could strengthen their competitive and financial advantage, either through a favorably priced trade in raw materials or
through an actual export agreement on the finished product.[3]

However, even if present political obstacles were eliminated,
Hirsch suggests that the overriding impediment to project implementation would be the provision of adequate financing, particularly for
ventures with a slow return on the initial investment. Thus, again,
we inevitably come full circle to the question of resources and mechanisms for ensuring their availability.

Pointing to the benefits of peace for Egypt, Professor Fred
Gottheil demonstrates in detail that Egyptians are better off economi-

cally since making peace with Israel, in spite of a cutoff in aid from fellow Arab states. Losses in aid were more than compensated for by oil revenues from the regained Sinai fields and from the Suez Canal as well as from increased tourism. Clearly, economic benefits alone could not have drawn Egypt to negotiate peace—and to imply this would deride the extent to which Anwar Sadat's search for peace in Jerusalem was a deeply felt effort to spare his people the death and sorrow of continued war with Israel. However, as Gottheil's chapter makes clear, the Egyptian government will have to forfeit, or "mortgage," significant aspects of Egypt's future development and betterment if it chooses to return to a war footing.

But it is to Abdul R. A. Meguid, former deputy prime minister for economic and financial affairs under President Sadat, that we turn for a deeply felt appeal for a Near East peace firmly based on mutual benefit, cooperative planning, and improvement in the quality of life in the region. Meguid reaffirms the call for wide participation in the peace process and for the establishment of a framework that would encourage cooperative endeavors.

Lest we leave the impression that a solution to these issues will propel the Near East to levels of economic progress heretofore unimagined, our book closes with the cautionary advice of Edward Azar, director of the Institute for International Development at the University of Maryland. He points out that traditional Western development assistance has failed to address the complex structural inequalities of Third World countries. Warning that the Near East is no exception, he cautions that any plan for regional development must address the capacity of a community to mediate between the needs of its population and the economic and political tensions of its environment. Because economic and development models are so often simplistic correlations between economic and political power—which assume that economic growth will, in and of itself, produce stability—Azar urges that development aid should be given only after detailed analyses of the structural interrelationships of the recipient societies have been made, and then only in ways that will reduce inequality and social violence. A narrow perspective could ultimately worsen, rather than improve, peaceful prospects for the Near East.

A Shared Destiny, for all its hope for the future, cannot offer one particular formula to solve the dilemmas of the Near East. While our authors concur that the best long-term approach to peace and development is through strong economic ties and cooperation, they do not always agree on the details of implementation. However, regardless of the framework, efforts to promote peace must be pursued as thoroughly and persistently as possible. It is in this spirit, then, that the following range of concepts and strategies for regional cooperation and development is presented.

NOTES

1. Among the in-depth analyses prepared for this project were detailed examinations of migration and population absorption projections for the West Bank and the Gaza Strip, as well as examinations of the opportunities for and constraints on economic growth and investment. See Bertram I. Spector, Sayyed Kayvan, Gary Keynon, and William Harvey, "The Economic Implications of a Middle East Peace Settlement," vol. 1: "An Economic Development Model for the West Bank and Gaza Strip," and vol. 2: "Migration and Population Absorption Projections for the West Bank and Gaza Strip," unpublished study prepared for the Agency for International Development, U. S. Department of State, December 1978. Estimating the likelihood of Palestinians to return to the West Bank and Gaza over a five-year period, and presuming 1979 to be the first year of a settlement, this study analyzes the prospects for providing employment, housing, education, and other essential services to these immigrants.

The study concludes, first, that as few as 104,000 and as many as 217,000 Palestinians would be likely to return to the West Bank and Gaza during this five-year period and, second—assuming a reasonable rate of growth—that the lower number of Palestinian immigrants could be absorbed with relative ease, while absorption of the larger number would require intensive foreign capital investment. However, taking into account "push and pull" factors affecting migration, as well as the continuation of current economic trends, the most probable population scenario through 1985 would involve low immigration and high emigration. To stop or reverse this projection, the study highlights a number of policy options to improve absorptive capacity.

Using a sector-by-sector approach, the study also determines the amount of expanded capital investment and assistance needed to absorb the projected inflow of Palestinian immigrants into the West Bank and Gaza. The construction sector, it was concluded, would require the greatest investment over the five-year period. Along with the public services, this sector can be easily expanded at a high growth level with the availability of substantial investment monies. Expansion of the agriculture sector, by contrast, will be hindered by scarce land and water resources, a situation that can only be reversed through massive capital investment for new crop cultivation techniques and irrigation technology. With regard to industry, the return on capital investment will be marginal in the short run owing to numerous "inadequacies." Trade, transport, and private services are predicted to grow at a rate consistent with the other sectors and with disposable income.

The study also concludes that the less developed Gaza Strip requires more foreign assistance and foreign private-capital investment than does the West Bank. Overall, however, the projection for the amount of foreign investment needed to sustain economic growth in Gaza is relatively small, since estimated immigration and emigration would be limited.

2. See Avigdor Haselkorn, Mordecai Kurz, and Abraham R. Wagner, "Trade and Economic Links in the Transition Phase: The West Bank and Gaza Strip," unpublished study prepared for the Agency for International Development, U. S. Department of State, November 1978. The study argues that it will be difficult to reverse or change the process of interdependence between Israel and the West Bank and Gaza, since the economies of these territories have already been highly integrated into Israel's economy.

3. The U. S. government has also been attentive to potential areas of cooperation between Israel and Egypt. In 1978, in response to a request from the Conference Committee on the International Security Assistance Act of 1978, the Agency for International Development commissioned "Regional Cooperation in the Middle East," a study by eight government agencies and ten private firms and individuals assessing prospects in a number of different sectors, including science and technology, transportation, telecommunications, water energy, industry and mining, and tourism.

2

THE EUROPEAN CONTRIBUTION

MAX KOHNSTAMM

In his <u>Memoirs</u> Jean Monnet quotes Antoine de Saint-Exupéry: "Man's finest profession is that of uniting men."[1] Looking about us today, we see nothing but disunity in the world, to the point where the danger of war seems to be returning. There is such disunity within the European Economic Community (EEC), with the member states so divided over paths to follow to overcome the worst economic crisis since the 1930s, that even the achievements it has already made seem endangered. Disunity exists, too, within our nations, rendering all government action difficult, and in some countries even impossible.

Faced with this disturbing situation, we should consider what the EEC can do for the consolidation of peace in the world and for the continuation of European construction, which is more necessary today than it ever was in the past.

Before doing so we should discuss Jean Monnet, who through the power of his imagination has changed the course of history on the European continent.

JEAN MONNET: HIS CAREER, VISION, AND METHOD

The son of a cognac merchant, Jean Monnet was born in Cognac, France, in 1888. He learned the trade very young and traveled the world selling his father's cognac.

On the outbreak of war in 1914, convinced that the outcome would depend on the organization of the war economy, Monnet managed to be given an audience at Bordeaux with the prime minister, René Viviani. Sent by him to London, Monnet devoted himself to setting up the Allied Executives, which represented in the economic sphere what the single command was in the military sphere. After the war, as deputy secretary-general of the League of Nations, he found solutions for the problems in Silesia and the Saar and directed the economic salvaging of Austria.

In 1923, because the Monnet firm was in difficulties and his father needed him, he again became a cognac merchant. After reorganizing the old house and becoming a banker, he again traveled the world; but after 1935, convinced that Hitler was leading the world to war, he became increasingly concerned by the lack of military preparations by the Western democracies. In 1938 Monnet was sent to Washington on a mission to President Roosevelt.

That journey began the mobilization of U.S. production to strengthen the Allies' potential, and the effort culminated in January 1941 with initiation of the U.S. Victory Program. At the outbreak of war Monnet was in London, once more organizing economic cooperation between France and the United Kingdom. In June 1940 he proposed to Churchill the total union of France and the United Kingdom. After Pétain concluded the armistice, Monnet pursued mobilization of the U.S. economy as a member of the British Board of Supply.

After the war, back in Paris as first commissioner for the Economic Reconstruction Plan, he laid the foundations for restoration of the French economy. Even during the war he had been convinced that, once it was over, it would be essential to offer tomorrow's Germany a place of total equality in Europe, and also that French industry, like any other modern industry, would need a large market. In 1950 he suggested to Robert Schuman the plan for a coal and steel community as a first step toward a European federation, chaired the conference drawing up the Treaty of Paris, and thereafter became president of the High Authority.

But when the proposal for a defense community failed in the French Chamber of Deputies, Monnet resumed his freedom and founded the Action Committee for the United States of Europe, which acted as a prime mover in the unification of Europe.

At the age of 89, he died at Houjarray in the house he loved so much. His funeral was attended by friends from all the EEC member countries and from the United States, among them the president of the French Republic and the chancellor of the Federal Republic of Germany.

Monnet's was an astonishing career, beginning as a brandy merchant and ending as the man behind the union of western European peoples. His <u>Memoirs</u> and an excellent, brief essay by Jacques van Helmont entitled "Jean Monnet comme il etait"[2] introduce an extraordinary man. Given Jean Monnet's great modesty, however, his <u>Memoirs</u> lack one vital element: the great warmth that radiated from him and inspired so much friendship and love in all who had the good fortune to know him.

When we speak of Jean Monnet's vision we must be cautious. For while it is true that the essence of his method always remained the same, from his work during World War I until the end of his life, it was applied to whatever job he faced without preconceived ideas. His vision developed and evolved, culminating in the conception of a European community whose compelling role was to give itself an organization that would transcend nations and frontiers.

A brief anecdote illustrates much about both the man and his ideas. In early September 1953, the Treaty of Paris had been in force for only one year, and in the course of that year the first common market in Europe—that for coal and steel—had been established. Monnet, back from one of his rare vacations, asked me to come to Bricherhof, his Luxembourg home. We walked in the garden while I reviewed what had happened during his month-long absence: we had started a program of constructing houses for miners; a problem had arisen over pricing of scrap iron; a few other matters had disturbed the calm of August. Suddenly, as he so often did during his walks, he stopped me, cut short the discussion of detail, and said: "Yes, yes, all this is very important, but what is our policy going to be towards the United States, and how are we going to deal with the Soviet Union?" Jean Monnet never despised details; on the contrary, he could go over endlessly those he judged important. His question, however, indicated that he saw the EEC not only as being indispensable for solving Europe's internal problems, but also as a means to achieve organized peace, "as a stage on the way to an organized world of tomorrow."[3]

Jean Monnet, who would have laughed if you had called him a philosopher, was a very great, profound humanist. His vision had no room for abstractions; all his political action was centered on the human being—the liberty, dignity, development, and responsibilities of the individual. Because this dignity presupposes equality between men and between nations, he always opposed any desire for domination. "Equality is absolutely essential in relations between nations, as it is between men. A peace based on inequality can have no good results."[4]

The method he applied to the successive goals he pursued was based on the conviction that in the modern world "where there was organization, there was real strength."[5] But organization ought to have as its object the common interest. Accordingly, the first essential was to identify that common interest. How? By drawing up a "balance sheet," a term appearing on almost every page of his Mem- oirs. (He writes, "Balance sheets of this sort have been milestones in my work: the strength of our fleets in 1916, of our air forces in 1940, of Allied and Axis military power in 1942, of the French econ- omy in 1945, and of the six-nation European Community in 1950.")[6]

These balance sheets should be the result of joint study, which was the opposite of conventional negotiations. "At no time must the study take on the character of a negotiation. It must be a common task."[7] Once drawn up, the balance sheet gave an "overall view," another term that turns up many times. It is the dynamics of both the balance sheet and the overall view, jointly developed, that changes the context in which a problem is posed. This change is nec- essary in order to solve problems that were insoluble in the old con- text, and is, therefore, what makes action possible.

In addition, any action calls for imagination and calculation, as well as an understanding of others and constant application to the task; for only those who apply themselves stubbornly to their task will see their chance when it comes. Finally, like a cognac producer, Monnet knew how to wait, how to have patience, for great actions are possible only when men are impelled by necessity.

What were, in his opinion, the obstacles that had to be sur- mounted in order not to lose "the race with international anarchy?"[8] To be sure, "without a doubt, the selfishness of men and of nations is most often caused by inadequate understanding of the problem in hand, each tending to see only that aspect of it which affects his im- mediate interests."[9] That is why the balance sheet and the presen- tation of the problem as a whole were essential.[10]

But the most formidable obstacle is the national egoisms ex- pressed by the requirement for and the use of the veto.

In the affairs of nations, coordination alone does not lead to a decision, and is therefore an inadequate method. That is why it is essential to create institutions to which people delegate the power to make decisions necessary in the common interest. Neither coopera- tion nor even great men can ensure that a lasting result will be achieved. "Nothing is possible without men: nothing is lasting with- out institutions."[11] Monnet described his ideas on institutions further when writing thus: "But men pass away; others will take our place. We cannot bequeath them our personal experience. That will die with us. And we can leave them institutions. The life of institutions is longer than that of men: if they are well built, they can accumu- late and hand on the wisdom of succeeding generations."[12]

One point is especially important in light of our situation today. Traveling at a very early age to the United States and Canada, Jean

Monnet learned the importance of the large market, of competition, and of free trade. But he never made it a dogma. On the contrary, experience also taught him very early the importance of organization for the economy. And he had no fear of government organization. After World War I ended, he struggled—though in vain—for an "organized peace."[13] He would have wished to keep the Allied Executives in existence, and he was fully in agreement with Prime Minister Clementel when the latter declared, "It is a complete illusion to hope to restore world equilibrium merely by means of the law of supply and demand."[14] Also after World War II, Monnet was convinced that renewal of the French economy called for a plan, but that the plan ought to be "concerned as much with orientation as with control."[15]

During negotiations leading up to the Treaty of Paris, he insisted that the High Authority be given the power, in the event of severe imbalances, to intervene in the market. And when the European Atomic Energy Community (EURATOM) and the EEC agreements were coming into being, he was interested particularly in the former, and in establishing a plan of action to be carried out under the supervision of the EURATOM Commission. As it happened, things went differently. But in Monnet's thought and action, the idea of organization played an important part in economic respects, too. What he sought was a proper proportion between organization and market forces, a proportion that would be different each time and that should be decided in accordance with the needs of the moment.

Having had the privilege of working at his side for more than a quarter of a century, I am faced today with the situation of our world and our EEC, both worried and full of hope, however contradictory that may seem. I am worried because I see our peoples, even within our nations, deeply divided over how to overcome economic difficulties and how to avert the threatening dangers of war. I am worried because I see that the construction of our peoples' union is no longer progressing. In fact, the very existence of what has been created, the European Common Market, is today threatened by the difficulty its institutions are having in responding to the most pressing problems of the day—namely, unemployment and inflation—and in giving Europe an industrial structure fit to meet the challenge of a world economy that is very different from what it was 25 years ago.

I am worried because the hope that a third world war might forever be avoided is gradually being replaced by despair. This despair threatens to block the imagination needed to find an answer "proportionate to the dangers which threaten."[16]

I am worried because I belong to the generation born during World War I and am haunted by the memory of our democracies' indifference to the rise of dictatorship, of their inability to surmount the economic crisis of the 1930s, and of the plague of unemployment without which Hitler would never have been able to seize power.

I am worried because I was, albeit for a few brief months, part of the world of concentration camps, and my memories of what went on there 40 years ago are, for me, still part of the present. It was there that I experienced what man is capable of doing to man. It was there that I learned it is possible to create circumstances in which men can no longer think of anything but their own survival. It was there that I became inculcated forever with both the horror of violence and the awareness of the weakness of our good intentions when they are not backed up by the law and by institutions to ensure that the law is applied.

I am worried, but at the same time I am hopeful. Why? Because in circumstances as threatening as today's, I saw how positive, imaginative action broke a vicious circle of hatred and violence and reversed what seemed to be the inevitable course of events.

Although in 1950, thanks to the Marshall Plan, our countries had begun to recover from the devastation of war, the towns of Germany—and many elsewhere—were still in ruins and our countries' productive capacity was barely level with what it had been 20 years earlier. In addition, these countries, still profoundly divided between victors and vanquished, were immersed in a cold war that threatened the barely reestablished peace.

At the beginning of May that year, Jean Monnet wrote to Robert Schumann with his thoughts on the situation:

> Whichever way we turn in the present world situation we see nothing but deadlock—whether it be the increasing acceptance of a war that is thought to be inevitable, the problem of Germany, the continuation of France's recovery, the organization of Europe, or the place of France in Europe and the world.
>
> In such a situation there is only one way out: positive, resolute action on a limited but decisive point, which brings about a fundamental change at that point and, step by step, changes the very terms of the problems as a whole. [17]

I had the privilege of taking part, first, in negotiations leading to the Treaty of Paris, and then in the setting up of the European Coal and Steel Community. During these negotiations—which, more than negotiations, were a joint search for solutions to the problems facing us—and while working at Luxembourg, I experienced a rebirth of hope and saw that the future was starting to dominate the past, wiping out hatred (which is always destructive), and transforming our memories of suffering into a constructive force.

I have discussed Jean Monnet because I am convinced that, today as in the past, his vision of the world can help show us the way, and that an understanding of his method can teach us how to go about the action that is necessary.

To ask what Jean Monnet would have proposed today would be to raise a hypothetical question, a kind of question he always refused to answer. Therefore, I do not suggest he would have made the proposals I want to submit. If my proposals are right, I owe it to what I learned from him; if not, then the mistake is mine.

THE LESSONS OF JEAN MONNET FOR BUILDING PEACE IN THE NEAR EAST

My first proposal concerns the action Europe should take in order to strengthen what was begun at Camp David and to consolidate peace in the Middle East. European action might have two aspects that would, of course, be intimately linked. The first would be to help in finding a solution for the problem between Israel and the Palestinians, because as long as that problem is not solved, the peace between Israel and Egypt will remain fragile, regardless of whatever efforts are made, and the danger of a new Middle East war will continue to threaten the world. The second aspect would be to help Egypt and Israel consolidate the peace resulting from the late President Sadat's historic visit to Jerusalem and the ensuing Camp David Agreement.

We all know how serious and numerous the threats to peace are today, and of course, that real peace among Israel, the Palestinians, and all their neighbors will not by itself guarantee the peace of the world. However, a Middle East peace would do more than solely eliminate one of the most dangerous threats to world peace.

Why? Because the gravest danger threatening us today is the fear that our problems cannot be solved peacefully, that in the end irrational and destructive forces will always overcome the weak power of goodwill and rationality. Wars are not always started intentionally. Certainly, Hitler started World War II intentionally. To a large extent, however, that war was the result, the continuation, of the first one. And there is convincing evidence that World War I was neither willed nor carefully planned, but that it simply happened, overwhelming nations and their leaders. The fault of those leaders had been to accept war as a possibility, to be unwilling and unable to break out of the vicious circle that imprisoned them and that finally led to the catastrophe of August 1914.

About the years before 1914, Churchill has written the following: "There was a strange temper in the air. Unsatisfied by material prosperity, the nations turned fiercely towards strife, internal or external. National passions, unduly exalted in the decline of religion, burned beneath the surface of nearly every land with fierce, if shrouded, fires. One might almost think the world wished to suffer. Certainly men were everywhere eager to dare."[18]

Real peace among Israel, the Palestinians, and the Arab nations would recreate hope—the most precious of all commodities—and would reestablish confidence in the creative power of peoples and their leaders to overcome the passions of the present, which are born out of the violence of the past.

Let us examine Europe's interest and responsibility in the conflict between Israel and the Arab nations, a conflict primarily between Israel and the Palestinians, both inside and outside Israel. I mention Europe's economic interest first because it is the most obvious. As we all know, our nations have allowed themselves to become utterly dependent on imported oil in a short span of 20 years. There is no excuse that this happened. Shortsightedness prohibited taking measures in time. In less than ten years, there is little chance—whatever temporary lull there may be in the demand for oil—of reducing this dependency to levels that can be considered reasonable in our interdependent world. In the meantime, any disturbance of peace in the Middle East, be it internal upheaval or war between the region's nations, threatens the flow of oil. In cases like the revolution in Iran or the Iran-Iraq war, Europeans can only hold their breath, try to remain neutral, and hope the danger will pass.

Renewed armed conflict between Israel and its neighbors would be a very different matter, for very probably it would turn oil into a political weapon. It is useless to say that oil should not be such a weapon, since we ourselves created the situation that made this possible, and crying over spilled milk will not help us. However, such a situation would mean Europe could not remain neutral. The EEC might be faced with a brutal choice between taking sides against Israel or being cut off from Middle East oil. To be cut off from Middle East oil might lead to an economic crisis endangering the delicate fabric of our societies. Yet, to take sides against Israel would be to betray compelling moral obligations that stem from our European history.

From the time of the destruction of the temple and the beginning of their exile, Jews have prayed for and dreamed of the return to Jerusalem. But the movement to turn this dream into a reality by recreating the state of Israel was born in Europe at the turn of this century. Political Zionism became a force impelled by the suffering of Jews, especially in eastern and central Europe. During World War

I, reasons of state contributed forcefully toward a beginning of the realization of Herzl's dream of a Jewish homeland in Palestine. Whatever assistance came from elsewhere, notably from the Jewish community in the United States, Zionism and the beginning of the return of Jews to Israel form a page in the book of European history.

Then came World War II when the unthinkable happened. Of course, it was Hitler and his henchmen who made it happen, but are we sure that more could not have been done to prevent it or to halt it while it was happening in our very midst?

For those who have not been there, it may well be impossible to imagine what it means to have survived Auschwitz, to mention only one of the places where the inconceivable became a reality. But we should never forget that to the survivors as well as to their children the past remains inexorably present. Only if we try to see the world through the eyes of those survivors and their children will we be able to help solve the conflict between Israel and the Palestinians.

However, Europe also has compelling moral obligations to the Palestinians. Therefore, we must try to look through their eyes, too. They did not contribute to the suffering that for numerous Jews made the recreation of Israel a necessity, an inescapable obligation to the millions that did not survive, the only conceivable road to a future. Palestinians cannot but see themselves as innocent victims of the actions of others, for which they bear no responsibility whatever. Moreover, deeply rooted democratic convictions, the basis upon which our societies rest, oblige us to recognize the Palestinians' right to have a home of their own, to take their destiny into their own hands, to decide themselves about their future. Furthermore, the destruction and suffering brought about by two wars have taught us that stable and lasting relationships between nations and peoples can only be built on the basis of equality, and that any attempt by one people to dominate another will fail in the end, in violence.

We are faced, then, not with a conflict between right and wrong, but with one pitching right against right, a conflict seemingly impervious to solutions because one party is marked—often literally marked in the flesh—by the memory of an unspeakable horror, and the other party is marked by present suffering. Whatever the economic advantages may be of living under Israeli occupation, they are of no matter to a people forbidden to be the master of its own destiny.

Let us try to put ourselves in the place of an Israeli, old or young. Remember that lonely Calvary; those long trains of cattle cars from Greece, from Italy, from France, from Hungary, from Czechoslovakia, from Belgium, from the Netherlands; the total destruction of centuries-old centers of Jewish civilization in Poland, in the Ukraine. How would you deal with those memories? Would you trust anyone's guarantee, anyone's force but your own? Would you not say to yourself, "If there ever be another Holocaust, then we shall not be sacrificed alone?"

Let us also put ourselves in the place of a Palestinian, old or young, forbidden to return to the land that was his people's for centuries, or living in occupied territory, which always implies being subjected to inequality. Are we sure we would abstain from acts of violence?

Conventional wisdom teaches us that the matters of borders, of security, and of reciprocal rights and duties must be settled before any future cooperation can be envisaged. But what if, at present, the weight of the past forecloses such a solution?

The Old Testament contains an illuminating story. When God finally decided he had to destroy Sodom and Gomorrah, he commanded Abraham, Lot, and their families to flee from those cities. Under no circumstances, however, should any of them look backward. If they should (and Lot's wife did), they would be transformed into pillars of salt—and that salt is a symbol of fruitlessness.

The only way to be liberated from the past is to have a vision of the future. Unless hope (a view of a future better than past and present) is introduced into the existing situation; unless the context, dominated for both parties by past or present suffering, is changed—it seems unlikely that a solution can be found. I doubt that pressure will pave the way to many concessions by Israel. Instead, it may well enhance Israel's sense of isolation and thereby strengthen resistance to any kind of so-called concessions. And in any case, unless there is something much more imaginative than pressure, the eventual solution may well turn out to be no more than an armistice, leaving Israel and the Palestinians in mutual fear and distrust that might well lead to new violence. Europe should, therefore, help both parties to establish a view of what the region's future in peace could be. Doing that would in no way deny the need to define borders and to deal with problems of military security. Efforts to do so must and will continue. However, creating a dynamic view of the future, showing what cooperation and the establishment of joint responsibilities for essential elements in the development of the region could do, may well be a precondition for the success of those efforts.

What would be the essential elements of a development plan encompassing Israel, the neighboring lands inhabited by Palestinians, and maybe some or even all of the other states surrounding Israel? Would water, energy, and food be decisive elements in such a plan? Studies made in the past, and some at present, will be of great help in finding the right answers to this and other questions. Thus far, however, these studies have never had the political backing necessary to become a force for peace. By pledging the full support of its intellectual as well as its material means to the development and execution of such a plan, the European Economic Community could procure such backing. Nothing would have greater weight than if the Council of the European Communities instructed the Commission of the European Communities to develop it. However, if for some reason this does not happen, then men and women with imagination, knowledge, and influence should undertake the job. They should work together with those Palestinians, Israelis, and citizens of Egypt and the Arab nations involved in the conflict who are willing to participate in a joint effort.

Before moving on from this subject, let me repeat one thing, in order to prevent any misunderstanding.

I propose to deviate from the conventional wisdom (settlement of issues first; then, possibly, cooperation), not because I do not recognize the necessity of fixing borders and determining rights and obligations. Today, however, the existing context, the weight of the past, prohibits the beginning of a real dialogue and thereby threatens to make the essential arrangements impossible. The only road that seems open is a road that—granted, under totally different circumstances—the nations conprising the European Economic Community have discovered together: to let the vision of a common future break the vicious circle resulting from the past.

However precious time may be in the explosive situation between Israel and the Palestinians—and therefore between Israel and the Arab world—such a change of context can occur only gradually. We should, therefore, also use our imagination to consolidate what has already been achieved: peace between Israel and Egypt.

Our nations jointly decided to participate in the international peace force that, upon Israel's final withdrawal from the Sinai, will serve to guarantee the frontier between those two countries. And our peoples participate in the peacekeeping forces now in southern Lebanon. Separating nations, delimiting boundaries, establishing security measures and international guarantees backed by a peacekeeping force —all these are certainly necessary. However, the wars Europeans fought against each other during this century have taught us one lesson: separating nations leads to a situation that should more honestly be called armistice rather than peace. And in a world where all the marvels of modern technology are also applied to the means by which nations can destroy one another, even a long-lasting armistice is simply not good enough.

Real peace presupposes the creation of a tissue of common interests, of regular contacts between political leaders, civil servants, leaders of labor and industry; a tissue so thick and strong that it will stand the dangerous pull of sometimes sharply differing perceptions and interests. Differing perceptions and interests will continue to exist between nations, just as they continue to exist between citizens of one country. But these tensions must be placed in a different context from the conventional one of international relations, relations that have not changed fundamentally since Thucydides described them as those in which the strong do what they want and the weak suffer what they must. Europeans have learned how this new context can be constructed slowly, by jointly organizing common interests and by establishing joint responsibility for their maintenance and development.

For the first time in history this process of change, set in motion by the power of Jean Monnet's imagination, has made war between our nations unthinkable.

President Mitterand has justly said that today our European Economic Community lacks spirit and soul. Would not assisting Egypt and Israel—and other peoples of the region—to go beyond separation and armistice toward the establishment of real peace, help us as well as them?

In his Memoirs, Monnet says that a common effort depends on common aims. [19] This leads us back to the balance sheet and the overall view, which must be developed together.

What has to be done to consolidate the peace between Israel and Egypt does not differ in kind from what must be done to change the context in which, today, a solution of the conflict between Israel and the Palestinians seems impossible. By far the best thing would be if it were one and the same operation. However, this decision is not for us to make, but for those directly concerned.

Ours, however, over and above the welcome decision taken by our governments to help in the buffer force between Israel and its neighbors, is the possibility (and it seems to me the obligation) to help bring them together.

THE EUROPEAN ECONOMIC COMMUNITY
BEFORE A TRANSFORMED WORLD

I have no suggestions for solving the many burning issues on the EEC agenda today, such as reform of agricultural policy, division of budget costs among European countries, or problems connected with the entry of new members. But I have learned from Jean Monnet that it is often useful, not to say essential, in solving problems confronting us, to take a step back, to take what seems a roundabout route to find the point where action is possible; and since action begets action, the problem becomes soluble.

In contrast, my second proposal is for a stocktaking that, in my opinion, has become necessary following the profound changes occurring since the creation of the European Economic Community and the takeoff of the European Common Market in the European and world economies.

It may be tempting to seek, through closer cooperation among European nations in international relations, a substitute for dealing with internal problems. But Europe's capacity to act in the world depends on its internal cohesion, which is threatened today by low to zero growth, inflation, unemployment, and monetary disorder.

Only in connection with the last problem has the EEC been able to find a partial answer. In response to the end of the system that arose from the Bretton Woods monetary accords, the so-called Snake (a rather loose monetary mate arrangement covering about half the EEC currencies) was formed. This Snake survived the oil shock of 1973 and, after a courageous initiative in 1977 by Roy Jenkins, then president of the Commission of the European Communities, was followed by a considerably more important arrangement: the European Monetary System. This system, however, remains unfinished, and serious discussions in the Council of the European Communities are continuing on its second phase. Furthermore, although Europe's common interest is obvious, no EEC policy toward the dollar exists as yet; and on the key question of national economic policy coordination, no progress has been made.

It is, however, even more serious that the present world economic crisis endangers the maintenance of the European Common Market itself. National measures such as industrial subsidies, taken under the pressure of social and political tensions, and scarcely disguised protectionism threaten to impede more and more the free flow of goods across our member states' borders.

Why is this happening, notwithstanding the general desire, declared time and again by our governments, to reinforce our union? The reason may well be found in the revolutionary economic and social changes that have occurred since the middle years of this century when the treaties of Rome and Paris were drafted. Let us try to identify some of these changes. Government expenditure as a proportion of each nation's gross national product (GNP) has vastly increased, as has in consequence the importance of government decisions and actions in the economic process. In the early 1950s, despite considerable state-led reconstruction efforts, government expenditure in the European Common Market countries ranged from 17 percent to 28 percent of GNP. By 1980 that share had increased from 44 percent to 59 percent, more than double the earlier figures. Wages in real terms—that is, after deduction of price increases—have trebled during the last 30 years, while the social security systems of European welfare states have established previously unheard-of safeguards against the hazards of unemployment, illness, and old age. It is no exaggeration to say that those who formerly rightly thought of themselves as proletarians, with physical strength as their only asset, now expect and often enjoy a level of income and a measure of economic security formerly only possessed by the privileged and propertied.

These attainments have already profoundly influenced, and will continue to influence, the way work is conceived and the place it is given in the perception of life. Another result of this immense leap forward is an increase in nonmaterial demands, such as those for more leisure, education, and culture, and for the enjoyment of an unspoiled environment: a concept of social growth in which the quality of life plays a dominant role is replacing the simpler concept of economic growth. And whereas the market can ensure the production of material goods, the provision of many elements of so-called quality of life demands governmental action.

Microchip-based production and products are creating another peaceful revolution, promising more and better goods and services produced with fewer resources. Yet the most important saving is in blue- and white-collar labor. The microchip is a boon to those who work, for it eliminates repetitive, often physically hard and dangerous work; but it poses a threat to employment and increases the speed of industrial adjustment. Nevertheless, the research-and-development effort essential for creating new employment in advanced industries remains almost entirely national, and the market for some of the most promising new industries is still solidly divided into separate compartments by national procurement measures and regulations.

Finally, energy, which was cheap and abundant in the 1950s and 1960s, is now forcing European economies to adapt to high prices and uncertain supply.

Another industrial revolution is taking place in the world outside. Until recently, Europe enjoyed a virtual monopoly over most industrial production. There were hardly any effective competitors, because Eastern Europe and the Third World had little or no production for export. Japan, only recently a major producer, at first concentrated on the U.S. market; and the United States, the only potential challenger, largely preferred direct investment over trade.

Advances in transport and communications have facilitated the rapid spread of technology, capital, and know-how, spreading manufacturing industries to the world at large. Thus Europe's monopoly of industrial production is gone forever. The blitzlike development of modern industry in the countries around the Pacific Ocean may well result in a shift of the center of gravity of the world's economy away from the Atlantic Ocean, a movement comparable to what happened to the Mediterranean-based economies at the beginning of the modern era.

Furthermore, a large part of the world economy is now in the hands of governments, not only in the communist world (including China), but also in a number of the so-called newly industrializing countries. Capital is allocated by governments according to industrial priorities set by them, while many of them also decide on wages and social security payments.

One consequence of this development is a change in the nature of commercial policy. Formerly it mainly concerned tariffs, and the Treaty of Rome, by turning the various national tariffs into a European Economic Community tariff, delegated decisions concerning this tariff to the EEC institutions.

Today, world trade is strongly influenced by other elements, such as credit policy, barter deals, or transfer-of-technology agreements. Since these matters have not been brought under the control of EEC institutions, the EEC, although it is the biggest single participant in world trade, is less and less capable of pursuing a consistent commercial policy.

Another consequence of today's mobility of capital and know-how, together with government fixing of the level of wages and social security payments, is that competition with the world outside the EEC often depends not so much on natural advantages as on the difference between the levels of these wages and social security payments. I am not able to draw any conclusion from this development, but it was this kind of competition that the authors of the treaty establishing the first European community—that for coal and steel—intended to prevent between industries of the member states.

During the last decade, European nations have found themselves faced with problems resulting from these revolutionary changes, and many of these problems have led to government action, taken independently. However, individual nations acting in isolation cannot find viable long-term solutions.

No one nation can hope to escape the dictates of a chaotic international monetary system. No one nation, however self-sufficient in energy, can escape the effects of an energy crisis that hits its partners. No one nation can, on its own, cope with internal and external industrial revolutions without putting at risk both its own economy and the functioning of the European Common Market itself.

As we saw earlier in this chapter, every time Jean Monnet was confronted with new and difficult problems, his first act was to take stock, to draw up the balance sheets that opened the way to innovative solutions.

The establishment of joint supply boards during World War I was an idea both simple and radical that imposed itself once the facts were faced squarely. Monnet used the same methods when he was deputy secretary-general of the League of Nations, and later in coping with the difficult and complex problems of financing railroad construction in China and mobilizing the U.S. economy before and during World War II.

A dispassionate analysis of the facts facilitated the reconstruction and renewal of the French economy. As chairman of the conference that drafted the Treaty of Paris, later as president of the High Authority, and finally as president of the Action Committee for the United States of Europe, Monnet followed the same method, convinced that once a problem's nature and the available means to deal with it were clearly analyzed, the necessary decisions would follow.

Confronted today by an unprecedented situation resulting from revolutionary economic developments both inside and outside Europe, the EEC needs a collective effort to establish a balance sheet. Most of the elements necessary for doing so already exist. I am thinking especially of proposals of the Commission of the European Communities in the execution of its so-called Mandate of 30 May. What still has to be done is to combine these and other elements in a coherent picture, thereby providing European political leaders, as well as leaders of trade unions and industry, with an analysis of the changed background against which their economic problems and the existing means of dealing with them must be set.

A joint effort is necessary to enable European nations to overcome their present difficulties. However, as Monnet pointed out, in order to secure such an effort one must first define the common objectives. That is why a balance sheet establishing common objectives and the existing constraints on their realization is necessary.

In 1983 the European Economic Community will celebrate its twenty-fifth anniversary. I could not think of a better way to mark that event than for the commission to present such a balance sheet. The European Parliament could make an important contribution to drawing it up through hearings that could help analyze the present situation and indicate measures necessary to overcome the EEC's present disarray.

If, for whatever reasons, the EEC institutions, beset as they are with pressing short-term problems, were unable to undertake this task, then it would be up to politicians, trade union leaders, industrialists, academics, and imaginative men and women to undertake the task. It is by no means rare that initiatives of far-reaching consequences have been launched in this way. Monnet's life and work provide us with examples.

Institutions, and delegation of decision making to them, are essential elements of Monnet's conception and method, and yet one may wonder why I have not made any proposals for strengthening existing EEC institutions.

One reason is to be found in the measures already proposed or contemplated by the Council of the European Communities and by the European Parliament. I am thinking especially of proposals to strengthen the European union, and of the task the European Parliament has set for itself as a result of the action of the so-called crocodile group: to work out changes to existing EEC institutions in order to give new vigor to the European enterprise. I fervently hope that these initiatives will produce the desired results.

The other reason is that although I am convinced of the necessity, I doubt whether it will prove possible to bring about the delegation of significant new powers to EEC institutions before a coherent view has been established of what has to be done to overcome our present economic difficulties.

Often today one hears the question whether, in a world so different from his, Jean Monnet's vision of a united Europe and of its role in the world is still relevant. The answer to the question depends on the imagination that our governments, and we citizens of Europe, can show in the face of the dangers that today are threatening peace just as much as during the cold war years, and in the face of the economic difficulties that are threatening the European Common Market itself.

It may seem illusory to you that providing a view of what their common future could be could break the vicious circle in which Israel and the Palestinians are caught today, or that Europe could be instrumental not only in helping to provide the buffer between Israel and Egypt but also in bringing these countries together in joint enterprises.

It may also seem illusory to you that the centrifugal forces that today threaten the very basis of our unity can be overcome by drawing up a "balance sheet," an overall view of the EEC's situation in a changed and still rapidly changing world. Nevertheless, as Jean Monnet wrote in his Memoirs, "Until you have tried, you can never tell whether a task is impossible or not."[20]

NOTES

1. Jean Monnet, Memoirs (London: Collins, 1978), p. 199.
2. Jacques van Helmont, Jean Monnet comme il etait (Lausanne: Fondation Jean Monnet pour l'Europe, Centre de Recherches Européennes, 1981).
3. Monnet, Memoirs, p. 524.

4. Ibid. , p. 97.

5. Ibid. , p. 49.

6. Ibid. , p. 127.

7. Ibid. , p. 89.

8. Ibid. , p. 82.

9. Ibid. , p. 83.

10. Ibid. , p. 83.

11. Ibid. , p. 304.

12. Ibid. , p. 384.

13. Ibid. , p. 71.

14. Ibid. , p. 75.

15. Ibid. , p. 258.

16. Foreign Minister Robert Schuman's Declaration of May 9, 1950, quoted from Bulletin of the European Communities 13 (May 1980): 14-15.

17. Jean Monnet, Memoirs (New York: Doubleday, 1978), p. 289.

18. Winston Churchill, The World Crisis, 1911-1914 (Port Washington, N. Y.: Kennikat, 1970), p. 188.

19. Monnet, Memoirs (London), p. 20.

20. Ibid. , p. 321.

3

NEAR EAST ECONOMIC DEVELOPMENT: THE MARSHALL PLAN REVISITED

NADEEM G. MAASRY

In three short years, from 1948 to 1951, the Marshall Plan played a major role in changing Western Europe from a continent in great political and economic danger to an area with great hope and on the verge of an economic miracle. When we look at Europe in 1983, it is difficult to believe how that rich, industrialized continent looked 36 years ago, shortly after the end of World War II. France, Germany, and Italy had been battlefields; as in Lebanon today, cities were destroyed and public facilities were in shambles. The continent's productive plant was in ruins. Millions of people were homeless, without work, and most important, largely without hope.

Political institutions were not in much better condition. Several European countries in 1947 were embarking on new democratic experiments after decades of dictatorship. Divisions both among and within countries were deep and, as many people thought, abiding. Communist parties were strong and threatening in Italy and France, while the governments in both countries were weak and often stayed in power for only months at a time.

Although these countries, now so prosperous, had histories of economic advancement different from and more promising than the Near East countries today, it is a mistake to think that their economic and political recovery after World War II was preordained or even anticipated. Many observers after the war thought the European countries might remain a long-term economic burden for the United States.

It is amusing, but also useful, to remember that even ten years after the war the Organization for Economic Cooperation and Development (OECD), the Marshall Plan organization headquartered in Paris, was developing special types of farm machinery for use on the steep slopes of the Alps. Why cultivate such marginal fields? Because many doubted that Switzerland, Austria, Italy, and other countries of the region would ever develop the export capacities to purchase food overseas to support their populations. The Marshall Plan played a catalytic role in the realization of the economic miracles that have since been achieved in Europe. It would be a mistake to believe that such miracles cannot also take place in the Near East. In this context, it is useful to reexamine the Marshall Plan experience for the mechanisms that underlay Europe's economic rejuvenation.

THE PURPOSE OF THIS CHAPTER

This chapter briefly reviews the setting and history of the Marshall Plan and considers elements of the Marshall Plan experience that are relevant to the development of a Near East fund with a substantial private investment component. Although the Marshall Plan was principally a government-to-government effort, it would be a mistake to overlook the fact that the private sector played a major role in assisting the European and U. S. leaders who organized it, and in responding to the framework for economic growth that it established. No effort in the Near East today will succeed economically or politically without mobilizing the enormous entrepreneurial talents and potential for capital formation of the business communities of the nations in the region. In Europe the Marshall Plan provided a framework for private initiative. It should be a major goal of foreign investors and business leaders to ensure that plans for Near East economic revival mobilize the full potential of business communities in the region. Government-to-government aid would help to put the physical and institutional infrastructure in place, but the private sector must be free to build on and within these structures.

Although the Near East is not Europe, the Marshall Plan is relevant to an effort that must be made in the Near East today. This effort must promote not only economic development, but also cooperation between erstwhile enemies and healing of internal divisions within many countries there. For the effort now called the Marshall Plan had as its principal objective not economic development alone, but use of the advantages of economic development to increase international political cooperation and to foster internal political moderation. People having the opportunity to compete and advance economically within a framework of stable legal institutions and international relations may well be less disposed to fight their countrymen and their neighbors.

One problem with examining the Marshall Plan for signposts in approaching Near East problems today is that the concept of a Marshall Plan is so often invoked in other areas. Politicians and writers often speak of a "Marshall Plan for the cities" or a "Marshall Plan for the American industrial heartland." In the United States, these calls are usually meant as appeals for federal monies. They overlook, by and large, the important nonfinancial, self-help, and multinational planning components distinguishing the Marshall Plan from the foreign aid efforts that succeeded it. These nonfinancial elements must be stressed because the Marshall Plan was not only, or even principally, a transfer of resources. It was a program that helped— indeed required—Europe to mobilize its own public and private resources. This, in short, is what a similar development plan for the Near East must accomplish.

However, economic development is not merely a question of resources. Many regions with resources are not developing, while other nations with apparently poorer prospects have been able to release and harness their peoples' energies to achieve better lives. An important lesson of the Marshall Plan is that economic development is an organic process requiring the full participation of the people of the countries involved. Perhaps this is what makes real economic development so threatening to nondemocratic leadership in many parts of the world. Europe has proved that economic development is a process closely and intrinsically linked to freedom and democracy, and it is important that this link be recognized in the Near East.

THE POLITICAL ECONOMY OF POSTWAR EUROPE

The political requirements of postwar Europe were not unlike the requirements of Near East countries today. Governments were unable and unwilling to demand greater sacrifices from populations burdened by the pains of World War II. These populations also were distracted, as are those in the Near East today, by vendettas from the past and by the nostrums of communists and others who blame economic difficulties on scapegoats or on the capitalist system, rather than on the objective realities of countries devastated by war.

In 1947 Europe, as now in several countries of the Near East, it was politically impossible for governments to build and rebuild productive capital enterprises solely on the basis of increased sacrifices by their citizens. Rationing, currency controls, and systems

of subsidies were the price paid in Europe after World War II for domestic political peace, a situation not unlike the one existing now in
Egypt, Israel, and elsewhere in the Near East. Food and other basics
were subsidized in many European countries after World War II,
even though incentives for agricultural and other investment were
diminished and inflationary problems were increased by such subsidies. Pressures to pour capital into food, housing, and other forms
of consumption rather than into factories and fertilizers had to be
accommodated by political leaders. Thus, the problem in Europe
then and in the Near East now was political: to develop agricultural
and industrial productive capacity for the longer haul without causing
short-term political upheaval, and to allow the gradual reduction of
unproductive subsidies to be replaced by fully competitive, self-sustaining economies. The Marshall Plan made this compromise between economics and politics possible in Europe in a democratic context. An investment fund for the Near East must also develop that
region's economy for the long term, while simultaneously recognizing
the political realities of the area.

THE ROLE OF A NEAR EAST INVESTMENT FUND

In creating a structure for a Near East investment fund, one
must keep in mind a number of factors from the Marshall Plan period.
First, private-sector investments must contribute to building
domestic political consensus in Egypt, Lebanon, Israel, and other
countries that might eventually join this multinational effort. Leaders
and people in the Near East, like those in postwar Europe, cannot be
expected to support foreign private investment, relatively liberal
economic systems, international economic cooperation, or development of democratic processes, if these do not contribute to a greater
sense of economic fairness and equity. Political stabilization and
political development require an increasing sense that societies and
their economies are becoming more just and that the opportunities to
satisfy legitimate economic and political aspirations are improving.
It is a mistake to believe that uneven development, in which
many members of the society do not participate, will be acceptable
politically even though it increases a nation's gross national product
(GNP). In Europe, postwar economic development narrowed the gap
between the wealthy and the poor. If only for political reasons, economic cooperation in the Near East must have a broad democratic
base of support. Many recent efforts to promote economic development in less developed countries are now widely recognized to have
widened the gap between rich and poor. Recent analyses have cited

a sense of growing inequality as a major problem in Egypt under the late President Anwar Sadat.

One way of responding to the problem of inequality may be to design a private investment fund for the Near East that specifically recognizes the importance of capital accumulation and job creation in the mercantile and small-business sectors of Near East economies. The small-business, trade, and service sectors are the ones that can ultimately contribute the lion's share of employment opportunities. A look at Lebanon in its prosperous years, or at Israel and its small businesses and industries, supports this thesis.

Second, early in the process of structuring a private investment fund, public and private participants should be encouraged to explore and "catalog" small-business assets and capabilities in the region's countries and to promote efforts to provide maximum incentives to this sector. One can borrow here from the Marshall Plan procedure whereby countries were required to prepare the so-called Paris Report issued in September 1947, which cataloged their assets as well as their needs. The Near East has a deep well of entrepreneurial talent, which a private investment fund must find ways to put to work.

Put another way, it is important that private foreign investors in the Near East help to modernize not only the industrial base of the region's countries, but also the mercantile, service, and quasi-handicraft sectors of the traditional society with which most of the region's people are most often in contact. Lebanon may be a good example of the capacity of small-scale business to create many jobs and to increase the connections between traditional and modern sectors of the society. Japan, of course, is a stellar example of a premodern agricultural, handicraft, distribution, and marketing economy that continues to expand and employ millions of people, while more advanced opportunities are created in new areas. It is vitally important to promote the health of older sectors of the economy that can employ millions, while simultaneously expanding and developing new activities.

In Europe after World War II, when much attention focused on rebuilding industry, it is clear that most new jobs were first created, as suggested above, in relatively traditional areas of the economy like trade and services. One major mistake in many non-European developing countries since the war has been the costly funneling of capital to large industries and to governmental marketing agencies that were incapable of absorbing these funds and putting them to productive use. In contrast, in countries like Lebanon, and in Europe and Japan, the older mercantile sectors of the economy have been encouraged to modernize, to contribute to capital formation, and most important, to continue to create jobs.

Third, a Marshall Plan innovation that might encourage development of smaller local business in the Near East is the use of counterpart funds. European governments were required by the terms of the Marshall Plan to set aside sums in their own currencies equal to the money they received from the United States to be used for local development projects. Such funds could be used in the Near East, for example, as the samurai pensions were in nineteenth-century Japan, as the seed capital for a whole banking system designed to develop local businesses, or at least as the local capital that many of these businesses could use to expand.

A fourth key role for a Near East investment fund, also based on the experience of the Marshall Plan, would be to encourage international cooperation as a specific condition of assistance to and investment in the fund. The sovereign nations of Europe were not able to go their separate ways without regard to the needs of the other OECD countries and their joint plans for greater economic integration. Both U.S. and European economic self-interest and idealism were important in this unusual limitation of sovereignty. Both U.S. and European idealism promoted economic integration. Jean Monnet and other European statesmen had long argued that economic integration could reduce the danger of war in Europe. Americans like Secretary of State George Marshall and his Marshall Plan director, Paul Hoffman, did not believe that the individual European countries could develop successfully without greater economic cooperation. And this is certainly the case in the Near East today.

The requirement of cooperation can further help political leaders in responding to domestic political pressures. In Europe, the requirement of cooperation gave politicians in the individual countries a strong argument to use with domestic groups wanting to increase their own advantages. Politicians were able to say to such groups, "Yes, we would like to help you, but the Americans and our Marshall Plan partners insist that we follow another course." In this way, the narrow demands of various agricultural, industrial, and commercial interests were made more manageable, although certainly not easily so. Greater attention was paid to efficiency and questions of scale, and less to domestic political pressures for investment aimed at achieving national self-sufficiency. The same pressures may be expected and the same antidote may apply in the Near East.

PRIVATE VERSUS GOVERNMENTAL EFFORTS

The Marshall Plan was essentially a government-to-government effort in which, in the beginning, private investment played hardly any

formal role. Extensive exchange programs for private-sector leaders and technical assistance to private enterprises were, however,
part of the plan's early efforts and should be considered in the Near
East context.

But a government-to-government approach was more appropriate in Europe than it is now in the Near East. The private sector in
Europe was relatively advanced and its ability to deal with government agencies and political leaders in a balanced way was not in question. This is not the case in several Near East countries today. The
private sector in these countries is weak and underrepresented in its
dealings with government. One of the most important roles to be
played by foreign investment and a foreign investment fund in these
circumstances is to strengthen the ability of local businesses to work
with governments. While it was possible to ignore the role of private
investment in Europe to some degree, it will not be possible to do so
in the Near East and still achieve the balanced and liberal development that is needed in the region. For example, balanced growth will
require development outside the larger cities, and in these smaller
centers the best tool of development will be small business leaders.

THE IMPORTANCE OF PROCESS

Most of those who have reviewed the Marshall Plan experience
emphasize the importance of process. While $13.3 billion of Mar-
shall Plan money was important to Europe, most agree that the plan's
sense of purpose, its requirement of cooperation, the flexibility of its
administration, and the commitment of European and U.S. leaders
were even more important. Moreover, the Marshall Plan contributed
to the development of European institutions: the European Payments
Union (EUP); the Organization for European Economic Cooperation,
which has become the Organization for Economic Cooperation and Development (OECD); the European Economic Community (EEC); the
European Coal and Steel Community (ECSC); and others. Many European political and business leaders received useful early experience
in Marshall Plan-related organizations, as well as in leadership and
business exchanges encouraged by the plan.

Commentators on the Marshall Plan note that many early economic assumptions of the plan were wrong and were abandoned, but
that the process continued. A first order of business for the creation
of a Near East investment fund with a strong private-investment component should, therefore, be the consideration of process. The government and business leaders of the countries involved should begin
early to assess their own assets, as European leaders did during the
summer of 1947 in response to Secretary of State Marshall's offer.

The first step is to mobilize the private-business, labor, and government leaders in each country to interact with those of partner countries. The foreign private-investor community should, as a condition of its full participation in this effort, insist that large and small businesses play an adequate role in the planning and discussion processes. Wide participation, as the Marshall Plan showed, is a requirement of economic development. Perhaps one day a Beirut Report, a Cairo Report, or a Tel Aviv Report will be as well remembered as is the Paris Report, which emerged from the summer of deliberation in 1947. Such a report, developed with full participation of business and government leaders in the region, could be the beginning of a process of Near East economic cooperation that, like the Marshall Plan, will develop the full economic potential of the participating nations.

4

ESTABLISHING THE PRECONDITIONS TO LONG-RUN DEVELOPMENT: EGYPT AFTER THE TREATY

FRED M. GOTTHEIL

Discussions of the difficulties Egypt faces with its Arab neighbors since signing the 1979 peace treaty with Israel sharpened after the assassination of Anwar Sadat. Egypt's political, psychological, and economic difficulties often appear so dramatic that one could easily forget its long-standing problems before the 1979 treaty. Somehow, in these discussions of Egypt's current hardships, its pretreaty economic history tends to be overlooked, even though to disregard that history is to ignore a major part of Egypt's thinking on the treaty issue.

The period 1948-77 had not been kind to Egypt or to the Egyptians. Their standard of life had hardly changed as the growing population pressed further on its severely limited land resources—as it had been for the past century—and the prospects for change, rhetoric aside, seemed as remote in 1977 as they were in 1877. Above all else, in this pretreaty era was the constant threat of war, which four times had broken into warfare, creating in its wake the enormous economic and human losses that such wars and war preparation can impose upon a nation.

Admittedly, Egypt was a decisive decision maker on the issues of war and peace. But as the Arab-Israeli confrontation continued into the 1970s, Egypt became less and less able to determine, on the basis of its own national interest, the pace and direction of the confrontation.

Egypt's increasing inability to dictate the character of the con-frontation—and its own realization of this inability—was dramatically illustrated in the diplomacy that almost brought into being the U.S.-initiated Geneva conference of 1977. The conference was designed to promote a comprehensive peace in the Middle East. But Egypt cor-rectly perceived it to be ill-fated, for it was clear then to Egypt and to Israel that no comprehensive interest existed among the Middle East confrontation states for such a peace. Under such a constraint, Egypt believed that it would be forced at Geneva to accept policy posi-tions on the confrontation issue that reflected more Syrian and Pales-tine Liberation Organization (PLO) interests than its own. Moreover, Geneva would have reestablished the Soviet Union as a major decision maker in the politics and life of the region, a circumstance that Egypt considered intolerable.

In short, Egypt was fearful that the outcome of such a Geneva conference would push it into a war it was unprepared and unwilling to fight. Sadat's response was the historic trip to Jerusalem in No-vember 1977.

THE ECONOMIC ISSUE

Whatever else Sadat's trip to Jerusalem represented, it demon-strated a shift in policy that conformed more closely to Egypt's long-run economic interest. Wars are expensive. Sadat was keenly aware of this elemental fact when he responded in a 1979 May Day speech to the Arab threat of cutting aid to Egypt by pointing out that while the oil-rich Arab states did provide Egypt with approximately $4 billion in grants and loans—essentially to underwrite the wars—the costs of these wars to Egypt exceeded $40 billion. We could quibble with the precision of these numbers, but not with their implications.

Moreover, in 1977 Egypt had little room for economic maneu-vering. The Egyptian economy started the year under quite unattrac-tive and dire circumstances. Even before Sadat's surprise visit to Jerusalem, total external capital funding for Egypt had fallen drama-tically—from $3.1 billion in 1975 to $1.9 billion in 1976. This cut-back denied Egypt its vital imports. Because of low demand elasticity for basic foodstuffs—imported food, among them—the consequent im-port cut fell disproprotionately upon imported capital goods. In turn, capital-goods shortages created industrial bottlenecks that forced gross domestic product (GDP) growth estimates to be revised down-ward. That is to say, while the world was experiencing one of the most dramatic distributive shifts of global income in recorded his-tory—primarily to the Middle East—Egypt was experiencing increas-ingly intolerable prospects for its economic future.

TABLE 4.1

Food Subsidies, Total Current Expenditure of the Central
Government, and Ratio of Food Subsidies to Total Current
Expenditure of the Central Government: 1974-79
(in billions of dollars)

Year	Food Subsidies	Total Current Expenditure of the Central Government	Ratio of Food Subsidies to Total Current Expenditure of the Central Government (in percent)
1974	329	825	39.8
1975	491	959	51.2
1976	322	1,335	24.1
1977	313	1,315	23.8
1978	423	1,629	25.9
1979	984	2,024	48.2

The evaporation of its external capital funding also meant that
Egypt would find it more difficult to service its short-term debt commitments. In an effort to address these critical servicing problems,
Sadat chose to cut further into the already decreasing food-subsidies
item in his budget and, at the same time, to raise taxes. The squeeze
on food subsidies during the mid-1970s is shown in Table 4.1. Both
subsidy levels and their percentage of the central budget declined.

This retrenchment policy quickly touched off the mass rioting
and antigovernment demonstration of January 1977. Sadat was forced
to suspend the austere budget and to rescind the food-subsidy cuts.
In retrospect, it was clear that the pretreaty "business as usual"
was no longer a viable economic option. The serious problems of
Egypt's underdevelopment had been left unattended during the confrontation years and even its short-term, stop-gap policies to get by from
year to year—which required increasing doses of external short-term
funding—were no longer working. In the pretreaty Arab world, the
rich were getting richer and the poor were getting into wars.

The Costs of GNP Forfeiture

The succession of wars that marked the post-1948 Middle East
had a devastating effect on the Egyptian economy not only in terms of

TABLE 4.2

GNP Estimates for Israel, Egypt, Syria, and Jordan, 1985
(in millions of dollars)

	100 Percent Conversion			30 Percent Conversion		
	n = a	n = 2.5	n = 5	n = a	n = 2.5	n = 5
Israel	18,902	35,052	32,574	18,802	22,841	22,324
Egypt	13,171	16,735	15,461	13,171	14,161	13,824
Syria	4,876	6,346	5,877	4,876	5,281	5,159
Jordan	1,432	1,815	1,678	1,432	1,538	1,502

its direct costs, but also—and perhaps of greater importance—in terms of the income and wealth Egypt forfeited during the war years. Although the assumptions that underlie the data in Table 4.2 are somewhat arbitrary (for example, the conversion rates of 100 percent and 30 percent), nevertheless the economic costs of Egypt's confrontation policy as shown in the table are rather imposing.

The estimates are generated by employing a simple variant of the Harrod-Domar model in the form

$$GNP_t = GNP_{(t-1)}[1 + r_t + \frac{(a_t - n_t)}{k}]$$

where GNP_t = the gross national product in period t; r_t = the rate of GNP growth at constant prices in period t; a_t = actual ratio of military expenditures to GNP in period t; n_t = the normalized ratio of military expenditures to GNP in period t; and k = the incremental capital-output ratio.

The burden of the Middle East confrontation to Egypt and to other participants is measured over the period 1975–85. In the case of Egypt, were the confrontation to persist throughout the 1975–85 period at the same level of military commitment that was actually undertaken in 1974—a_t = 1.8 percent—then, ceteris paribus, Egypt's 1985 GNP would have been $13.171 billion. If, on the other hand, during the 1975–85 period, Egypt would have been able to reduce its ratio of military expenditures to a normalized 5 percent—n = 5—and at the same time convert the resources released from the military to productive investment, then with k = 3, Egypt's 1985 GNP would have been $15.461 billion. In other words, the cost to Egypt of maintaining the confrontation at mid–1970 levels is reflected in a forfeiture of real 1985 GNP of ($15.461 billion - $13.171 billion) = $2.29 billion.

This $2.29 billion represents not an accumulated stock over the 1975-85 period but, rather, the loss of GNP incurred in 1985 alone. The significance of this forfeited GNP is that, with the mid-1970 confrontation levels sustained, annual GNP losses continue to grow. Egypt's GNP potential becomes crippled year after year.

The Costs in Earning Capabilities Forgone

The 1967 Arab-Israeli war not only produced for Egypt the territorial loss of the Sinai, but also created severe dislocations for its western Suez population. The cities in the Canal Zone, with its approximately one million inhabitants, were the major victims. The zone's major industries including its oil refineries were destroyed. The economic costs of these dislocations were registered not only in the complete loss of the zone's productive capacity, but also in the financial outlays that were required to support the internal war refugees.

Loss of the Sinai represented for Egypt a considerable loss of its export-earning power. Egypt's newly discovered oil resources were situated in the Sinai and Gulf of Suez regions. The 1967 war pushed Egypt completely out of the Sinai with the consequent loss of its oil potential. And the continued confrontation politics that followed the war made oil exploration and production in the Gulf of Suez region—still in the hands of Egypt, but well within a future war zone—less attractive to both private and government investors. Moreover, the Suez Canal, one of Egypt's few high value-added sources of export earnings, was made impassable by the war and, with Israel on its eastern bank, unusable in its aftermath.

In other words, by sheer force of geography, much of Egypt's export-earnings capacity—oil and canal—was dependent upon peace with Israel. In an atmosphere of continued confrontation, these revenue-generating sources could never fully realize their potential.

Table 4.3 illustrates this potential. Prior to the treaty, in 1974, the export revenues from Egypt's oil, Suez Canal dues, and tourism—also a peace-related item—combined to a $530 million total. The Sinai under Israeli control, of course, contributed nothing; neither did the Suez Canal, which was in disrepair and closed to traffic. Egypt's Gulf of Suez oil operations contributed $104 million.

In contrast to previous years, the 1980 data represent Egypt's peace harvest on the three items shown in Table 4.3. The return to Egypt of the Israeli-developed Alma fields in the Sinai contributed over 30,000 barrels per day (b/d) to its 600,000 b/d total produced in the Gulf of Suez region. Export revenues from these combined fields were $2.2 billion in 1980. In addition, resumption of traffic through

TABLE 4.3

Actual and Anticipated Earnings from Suez Canal Dues,
Oil Exports, and Tourism, 1974-86
(in billions of dollars)

Source	1974	1979	1980	1986
Suez Canal dues	—	0.60	1.00	1.20
Oil exports	0.10	1.30	0.70	5.50
Tourism	0.43	0.65	2.20	2.80
Total	0.53	2.55	3.90	9.50

the Suez Canal contributed another $1 billion. Tourism, too, showed
substantial improvement. By 1980, with Western tourists accounting
for an increasing share of the market, the tourism industry contributed
$700 million. In total, Egypt earned $3.9 billion in 1980 from these
sources alone. The 1986 estimates shown in Table 4.3 are derived
from the October Working Paper, a 1974 official document that projected national income data for 1986. The $9.5 billion estimate may
be too optimistic, but it nonetheless reflects Egyptian thinking, if not
potential, on the economic advantages of the peace. In other words,
Egypt's 1977 decision to move in the direction of peace and away from
continued confrontation was not without considerable economic expectation and realization.

Measured against these treaty benefits are the adverse effects
on Egypt's balance of payments of the economic sanction taken against
Egypt by the Arab governments in response to the treaty. The very-
much-talked-about, but very-difficult-to-assess, grants and loans
offered bilaterally and through intra-Arab multilateral structures,
such as the Gulf Organization for the Development of Egypt (GODE),
officially ceased. On the other hand, the incomes earned by thousands
of Egyptians working in the Arab states that provide considerable remittances to Egypt—$2 billion in 1979—remain unaffected. Also un-
affected are the relatively minor Arab direct investments—$150 mil-
lion in 1979.

In retrospect, Sadat's 1979 May Day speech contrasting Egypt's
$4 billion of grants and loans from the Arab states against its own
confrontation expenditures of $40 billion may actually have been a sub-
stantial understatement of the real net economic benefits that the
treaty afforded Egypt.

THE ARAB CONNECTION: KHARTOUM TO BAGDAD

Notwithstanding the measured treaty gains described above, the immediate consequences of the oil-rich Arab states' 1979 decision in Bagdad (to end all loans, deposits, and availability of banking facilities to Egypt directly, and to refrain from participating indirectly through an assortment of Arab bank funds and other financial intermediaries within the Arab League to aid Egypt) produced for Egypt a setback in its efforts to reduce the deficits in its balance-of-payments accounts. For whatever else may have been happening, the structural problems that chronically produced Egypt's deficits on current accounts continued unabated. However attractive these peace-related sources of revenue may have been, Egypt could scarcely afford to lose a capital-funding supplier. No doubt Egypt hoped to feed from both troughs. But that option was denied and, forced to choose on purely cost-benefit grounds, it made the more reasonable choice. The 1979 Bagdad Agreement clearly illustrated the precarious state of Egypt's international economic relations. Arab unity arguments aside, it showed how Egypt's new and growing Arab financial connection created for Egypt a condition that compelled it to pursue policies not in its own interest.

Actually, Egypt's Arab financial connection had been of recent vintage. Prior to 1967 Egypt had received no support from its Arab neighbors, with the exception of marginal contributions from Kuwait. Even as late as 1967, the Arab commitment to Egypt that originated in the Khartoum Agreement (resulting from the 1967 meeting of Arab foreign ministers in Khartoum for the Fourth Arab Summit Conference) was no more than $250 million annually, a sum meant to represent Arab compensation to Egypt for the Suez Canal revenues lost as a result of the war and the decision not to reopen it. During the period 1967-73, these contributions remained minor compared with the loans and grants offered to Egypt by the Soviet bloc nations.

The Arab connection developed in strength only after 1973. In the immediate aftermath of Egypt's participation in the 1973 war against Israel and as a show of good faith, Saudi Arabia, Libya, and the Gulf states provided Egypt with $750 million in grants and $352 million in short-term commercial bank borrowing. In that one year, these sums dwarfed completely the Arab states' Khartoum commitments and ushered in the new Egyptian-Arab relationship. These grants and loans, it should be noted, also date to the beginnings of the Organization of Petroleum Exporting Countries (OPEC) revolution.

In the following year, 1974, the Arab grants totaled $1.26 billion and provision for short-term commercial bank borrowing reached $585 million. In 1975 Egypt received $988 million in grants, but an

TABLE 4.4

Oil Revenues of Saudi Arabia, Kuwait, United Arab Emirates,
and Qatar, 1972-76
(in billions of dollars)

	1972	1974	1976
Saudi Arabia	3.107	22.600	33.500
Kuwait	1.657	7.000	8.500
United Arab Emirates	0.551	5.500	7.000
Qatar	0.225	1.600	2.000
Total	5.540	36.700	51.000

additional $1.4 billion was offered in the form of medium- and long-
term deposits in the Egyptian Central Bank. In 1976 grant assistance
fell to $625 million. The bulk of such assistance came from Saudi
Arabia and Kuwait. Libya, which had been until 1973 a major donor
under the Khartoum Agreement, completely cut its aid to Egypt as a
result of political differences. Table 4.4 puts these grants into perspective.

In 1976 the Gulf Organization for the Development of Egypt
(GODE) came into being, combining assistance from Saudi Arabia,
Kuwait, Qatar, and the United Arab Emirates. In 1977 GODE pro-
vided Egypt with $1.725 billion in aid and, apart from the GODE total,
Egypt received $825 million in short-term bank borrowing.

The replacement of Soviet bloc by Western and Arab aid was
thus dramatic and virtually complete. The Soviet connection, developed over a 16-year period, was relatively minor by 1975. In 1975
the Arab states already accounted for 57 percent of all of Egypt's loans
from governments. Western aid accounted for an additional 25 percent with the Soviet bloc representing the remaining 18 percent.

But these massive aid inflows were still insufficient to cover
Egypt's external deficits. Egypt's nonmilitary medium- and long-term
debt in 1976 was $5.86 billion, which represented 42 percent of its
GDP. Compare these figures with the 1973 debt of $2.49 billion,
which represented 26 percent of its GDP.

In spite of the magnitude of Arab aid, it was still less than Sadat
expected and considerably less than Egypt required. In an address at
Alexandria University in July 1976, Sadat pointed out that the $2 bil-
lion assistance from GODE was far short of the $10 billion to $15 billion required. Sadat had in mind long-term economic development

when he said, "I say to our good friends, with all the gratitude, recognition and respect that we owe them, that the Fund must take a different form than that which they want it to take. . . . I hope our friends will not be upset over this."

Although the Arab totals, bilaterally and through the GODE, were partially servicing Egypt's growing annual deficits, they were considerably less than those lost opportunities associated with Egypt's own redevelopment of the Suez Canal and Gulf of Suez regions (including oil), with the resumption of commercial traffic through the Suez Canal, and with the development of Egypt's tourist industry. In other words, the Arab aid, fixed as it was to the maintenance of a Middle East in confrontation, was to Egypt in 1977 more of a long-term problem than it was a solution. For to satisfy Arab insistence on maintaining the confrontation levels meant not only to forfeit these self-generating and potentially much richer sources of capital funding, but also and perhaps even more important, by having to accept the confrontation status quo, it meant as well that the fundamental problems besetting the Egyptian economic system would continue to be relegated, as they had been throughout the more than 30 years of the confrontation, to a second-order level of priority. To redirect Egypt's energies and resources to such fundamental economic concerns required, as Sadat understood, a much different kind of Arab connection. In this respect, Arab aid even at its peak levels was highly inadequate, much too directed toward short-run financial adjustment problems, and as the Egyptians learned quickly, far too capricious.

WHERE DO WE GO FROM HERE?

Egypt's economic needs in the 1980s, as they did in the 1970s, require a steady, reliable stream of massive capital funding over a reasonably long gestation period that can trigger the economy into and beyond a self-sustaining takeoff level of development. This can be done, and with proper funding the chances of success are high. Egypt has the human capital required to undertake such an enterprise. Sadat identified the problem and the needs when he introduced the concept of a so-called New Marshall Plan in 1978. Sadat then spoke of $15 billion over a five-year period, but what he had in mind was the initial stage. Clearly, the problems besetting Egypt call for strategies that can be developed only over decades. Essentially, Egypt must bring into balance its demographic and economic capacities.

The demographic problem is strikingly illustrated in Table 4.5. Malthusian fears appear justified in the Egyptian case. While population increased from 9.715 million in 1897 to 37.772 million in 1975—

almost a fourfold increase—the cultivated areas increased from 4.943 to 6.50 feddans. The cultivated area available per person, as a result, declined from 0.53 feddans in 1897 to just 0.17 feddans in 1975. Even if multiple cropping is considered—growing more than one crop per year on a feddan of land—the results are still dismal. Crop area (the number of crops per year times the number of feddans) per capita declined from 0.71 in 1897 to 0.29 in 1975.

Moreover, the population pressure appears to continue unabated into the 1980s and remains for Egypt its most formidable obstacle to economic betterment. Egypt's 1979 population was estimated at 41.2 million; its annual rate of growth is approximately 2.8 percent. In contrast, Egypt's production of basic foodstuffs has grown at an annual rate of 2.0 percent. The simple but devastating result has been that Egypt's ability to feed its own population, measured in terms of per capita availability of domestic food, was approximately 10 percent lower in 1979 than it was 20 years earlier.

This population pressure on the land has also produced considerable out-migration. Many of the most energetic and productive members of Egypt's labor force have quit the country completely by reestablishing themselves as temporary workers in Arab and European countries. While they provide a vital flow of annual foreign earnings through their remittances to Egypt, they represent a critical loss of productive manpower. A considerable migration has also occurred from rural areas to urban centers within Egypt. Cairo has become the major repository, with a 1979 population exceeding eight million. The basic reason for this unstemmed migration is economic: urban real-wage rates, although declining throughout the 1970s, were still 3.3 times the level in agriculture in 1977.

TABLE 4.5

Population, Cultivated Area, Cultivated Area per Capita,
and Crop Area per Capita, 1897–1975

Year	Population (millions)	Cultivated Area (million feddans)	Cultivated Area per Capita	Crop Area per Capita
1897	9.715	4.943	0.53	0.71
1917	12.715	5.309	0.41	0.60
1937	15.921	5.312	0.33	0.53
1966	30.079	6.000	0.20	0.34
1975	37.772	6.500	0.17	0.29

However sizable private foreign investment has been, it remains confined principally to oil, hotels, and other forms of real estate. In other words, it is concentrated in areas that have proved records of yielding high, quick returns. Sadat's Open Door Policy notwithstanding, such private funds cannot be expected to locate in the infrastructure formations that are designed to restructure Egypt's agricultural and industrial sectors.

To put into balance Egypt's demography and economy, the massive, long-run external capital funding that is required must be directed toward programs to increase agricultural productivity; toward programs to build satellite cities around Cairo and in the delta region to ease the population pressure on Cairo and, at the same time, to create in these proposed satellite cities industry that can both generate employment and take advantage of the expanding Cairo and satellite markets: and toward programs to improve the basic municipal services in Cairo itself, that is, the expansion, repair, and provision for proper maintenance of telephone, water, and electricity facilities without which the city becomes increasingly unlivable and unproductive.

Such a massive capital and human commitment would mark only the initial phase of Egypt's development path, for it does not follow that raising investments to the levels and direction proposed would necessarily produce the changes in real output that investment models typically describe. Development—as distinct from growth—implies predesigned shifts in Egypt's population with the consequent investment requirements for housing, schools, health facilities, road networks, sewage systems, and other formations associated with the development of human capital. These in themselves are necessary but not sufficient conditions for economic growth. They form the foundation for the more attractive prospects that would become available for private investment.

Egypt took the first major step in this positive direction in 1977. Sadat's trip to Jerusalem, which developed into the 1979 peace treaty with Israel, signaled Egypt's clearsightedness in identifying properly its long-run economic interest. Anwar Sadat's death has not altered his government's determination to seek for Egypt the fruits of peace. The terrible costs of war on a society facing such severe demographic and economic problems, combined with the proved economic benefits of four years of peace, are incentives for continuing the process Sadat began.

5

AFTER SADAT

ABDUL R. A. MEGUID

To the majority of Egyptians, Anwar Sadat's peace initiative at Camp David is not really a treaty or history to be told to our children. It is a philosophy, a way of life, a way of thinking. It is a process of thought that needs to be proved effective in changing the attitude of mankind from one of confrontation to one of cooperation and cordial achievement of a peace treaty.

President Mubarak has pledged sincere and dedicated efforts in the pursuit of peace. He believes, along with the Egyptian people, that peace is a strategy, not a tactic; that Egypt will follow the peace process as outlined in the Camp David Agreement and in the treaty with Israel; and that it is possible to go beyond this achievement to work in mutual cooperation.

REDEFINING THE WORD PEACE

Peace is not just a cessation of hostilities; it is a viable economic proposition and a stage toward mutually beneficial interdependence. In seeking international support for the concept of development, the conventional definition of peace should be discarded for one that is more encompassing.

Debate continues over which party sacrificed more at Camp David. Although both Egypt and Israel have given a great deal, we

47

must remember that peace is not a zero-sum game; however courageous and noble the cause, it takes two to make peace, and regardless of what either nation gave, both sides received more in return.

INSTITUTIONALIZING PEACE

What is needed at this juncture in history is a pioneering effort
to institutionalize the spirit of Jerusalem, the birthplace of Jesus and
the city visited by many people, including Anwar Sadat. The institutionalization of peace will facilitate continuation of a momentum that
must not stop. Such a task would take tremendous courage, foresight,
dedication, and tenacity. The institutionalization process needs to be
reinforced and it must have a following, involving people from all
over the world, not only in the United States, Europe, and the Near
East, but also in universities, among educators, writers, scientists,
artists, and all who strive for peace. The institutionalization process
needs to be felt by as many people as possible.

The momentum created by President Sadat's trip to Jerusalem
must be reinvigorated, and in order to do so, the horizon of peace
needs to be widened. At present, Egypt and Israel are the principal
recipients of funds from the Agency for International Development.
However, it is important to think not only in terms of Egypt and Israel
but also in terms of wider circles. The Palestinians, Jordanians,
Syrians, Lebanese, Iraqis, Saudis, and Kuwaitis must all be included.
The circle must eventually encompass countries from Iran to the
Yemens, and beyond into the Sudan and Somalia. All these countries
are participants in the same game, whose objective is not for any one
to win at the expense of the others, but for all to become winners.

A development mechanism for the Near East and beyond would
represent an initiative of no lesser importance and significance than
the peace initiative itself. Such an effort would require substantial
funds, dedication, technology, and persistence. This mechanism, in
whatever form it can be established or conceptualized, should not reflect the needs of any one country, but should relate to the needs of
the whole region. The areas of action and the intensity of action in
each direction need to be examined in order to find a solution that will
fulfill all who share in the vision of peace.

Peace and its expectation, while not synonymous with prosperity,
create conditions of stability that enable prosperity to evolve. Already
Egypt has clearly benefited from the peace process. In the years following President Sadat's Jerusalem initiative, peace has brought
Egypt a sense of fulfillment, achievement, and purpose, which has,
for example, made it possible to explore for oil. The balance of payments also turned from a deficit to a surplus.

ments also turned from a deficit to a surplus. Egypt can now rely more heavily on loans from donor countries. This is a source of strength. Combined with the balance-of-payments surplus, the enhanced ability to borrow allows Egypt to mobilize additional resources both at home and abroad. This, in turn, accelerates the development process beyond the country's autonomous resources. The fact that Egypt's economy has progressed this far in so few years is significant, because a healthy partner is an important partner.

The balance-of-payments surplus and the general improvement in the economy benefit Egypt psychologically as well. For the first time since 1960, the minister of finance does not have the right to issue treasury bills without the parliament's approval, a constraint that ensures a certain degree of fiscal responsibility. The minister of finance now needs to achieve the objectives, targets, and revenues that are included in the budget; he is also obligated to minimize expenditures or maximize the development process within the bounds of economic wisdom and proper management. The parliament and the Egyptian people now know that the psychology of inflation and the psychology of budget deficit must not be allowed to erode the cabinet's credibility in terms of controlling prices and maintaining a wage-price relationship that can be acceptable to the lower 40 percent income group or, indeed, to all the fixed-income groups in Egypt.

That type of point must be made throughout the Near East, and of course, Egypt is fortunate in getting the additional revenues to make it possible. People must know it is essential for the country to fight inflation. The budget is designed in large part for that purpose. The budget, in a certain respect, is not different from the Camp David process, for it is the same tool with which the psychology of the population can be affected. They are similar in that they create expectations of stability. When the Egyptian people went to the airport to receive President Sadat after his visit to Jerusalem, they illustrated Egypt's sudden change from having had a war-oriented generation for the past 20 years to having a peace-oriented generation at the present. Who could have imagined this would happen? The depth of feeling of humanity is something that cannot be switched on and off, but the use of appropriate psychology—the use of acupuncture if you will, to know where to put pressure and where to have the maximum effect of a given action—is perhaps the type of art that needs to be refined by all those interested in fostering peace and cooperation.

President Mubarak is aware of problems arising from population growth, redistribution of income, and subsidies, and he has the political courage to pursue reform. Indeed, he has opened all these issues for discussion. The fact that he is willing to listen to the views of others is one of the brightest aspects of Egyptian economic reform.

Egypt not only believes in peace and is willing to fight for it but is determined to be strong enough to defend it. However, Egypt's strength will come from more than machine guns and aircraft; it will come from the inner fabric of society and from a structurally reformed economy. Egyptians recognize their country's problems, but must face them without hesitation or reluctance. President Mubarak is prepared to do this.

THE PRINCIPAL PROBLEM IN THE NEAR EAST TODAY

Erosion of the social fabric of society is pervasive throughout the Near East as well as on its periphery, disrupting the whole region in unimaginable and unforeseeable ways. Khomeini's efforts and his impact on Arab and Muslim countries, as a primary example, are something to be feared. Unraveling of the social fabric causes the decline of Middle East civilization itself. This process occurs when institutions are increasingly unable to maintain these societies and when society ceases to respect common values and shared goals. The only option to stop this disease from spreading is to act—and to do so fairly quickly.

GOING BEYOND THE INVESTMENT CAPABILITIES OF INDIVIDUAL COUNTRIES

Egypt currently invests 25 percent of its gross national product annually in development projects. But this, combined with trade subsidies, is not the answer, for it inherently reflects an abnormal situation. Neither can it cement a structure between nations. The answer is to widen the underpinnings of peace structured on a regional basis. The example of joint fertilizer production is exciting, as is joint potential for textiles and clothing.

Such a concept for development requires projects that are selected because they are part of a program of action, projects that are integrated not only with each other and within individual societies that will absorb them, but also within a larger, newly interdependent society. The capability exists to create an institution dedicated to continuously identifying these types of projects, working out their viability, and assembling them into a comprehensive development plan for interdependence and mutual cooperation. Criteria for this comprehensive development process should include the four points explained below.

First, regional projects are not necessarily interchangeable with national projects. Any particular project must be part of a larger group of projects, where both parties benefit and nobody really loses anything. Institutional support for this process must be carefully designed, with echoes in all participating countries.

Second, it should be understood that no matter how attractive they appear on paper, nonviable projects are actually a liability to interdependence, for they can be a source of dissatisfaction and conflict. Especially at the beginning of the interdependence process, the projects that are selected must be capable of repaying their capital costs.

Third, the link between interdependent projects and availability of their benefits to the entire region must be strengthened. Projects should not have marginal value but should be capable of contributing to the economies of all participating nations, as might be the case with a new power station.

The fourth criterion can be called complementarity, whereby projects cement a development process along a path of integration and mutually beneficial interdependence. But complementarity is not to be confused with specialization, whereby two countries focus on different activities that are subsequently linked for their mutual benefit, as in the case of a textile project.

A new definition of peace between Israel and Egypt or their neighbors means that each will select projects with genuine concern for the needs of the other. This definition of peace goes beyond our present capacity to sustain it. Because existing international aid meets only the most immediate of needs, an additional mechanism is required for the infrastructure of interdependence. What is needed now is a program of action that goes beyond the philosophy of aid to individual countries, and that creates a framework for a development commitment to the entire Middle East.

6

EGYPT AND ISRAEL: PATHS OF COOPERATION

ZEEV HIRSCH

This chapter examines some of the problems involved in pursuing economic cooperation in the Middle East, using Egypt and Israel as a case study.

Bearing in mind that the long and bitter Arab-Israeli conflict has few, if any, economic causes, it would be rather naive to expect the prospects of peace to be perceptibly brightened by the lure of economic gains. Economic considerations must, at this stage of the peace process, assume a subsidiary role at best. Once breakthrough is achieved on the political front, however, economics are bound to figure more prominently in the peace process.

Considering that any economic intercourse inevitably contains elements of conflict, it is important to make sure that the initial transactions in which the parties engage offer an acceptable trade-off be-

This chapter is based partly on material for a book, The Economics of Peace Making—Focus on the Egyptian-Israeli Situation, written with Ruth Arad and Alfred Tovias and to be published by Macmillan for the Trade Policy Research Center of London in 1983. The financial contributions of the Tel Aviv University Project for Joint Economic Development in the Middle East and of the Samuel Rubin Research Fund in Middle East and Developing Countries are gratefully acknowledged.

tween these conflicts and economic gains. The approach developed in this chapter seeks to contribute toward this end.

The first section outlines some short-term political considerations that, in my view, will remain valid even after the war in Lebanon, which will undoubtedly have a profound influence on the Arab-Israeli peace process. Next, long-term prospects are examined. The section introduces concepts such as vested interest in peace and optimal interdependence, which ought to figure prominently in the consideration of policy makers concerned with developing economic relations with recent or potential enemies. In succeeding sections, these general concepts are examined within the specific context of the Egyptian-Israeli peace process and are illustrated by three case studies involving the textile and clothing, fertilizer, and cement industries. Some policy implications are considered in the concluding section.

SHORT-TERM PERSPECTIVES

An analysis of the potential for economic cooperation between Egypt and Israel must distinguish between the short run and the long run.

In the short run, development of economic relations is constrained by political considerations, including the recent war in Lebanon and its aftereffects, the lack of progress on the autonomy issue, and the refusal of other Arab countries to join in the peace process. These factors combine to inhibit expansion of Egyptian-Israeli economic relations and prevent them from reaching what might be termed their natural level.

It is unlikely that economic considerations, especially those pertaining to lost opportunities from failure to realize the potential gains from bilateral trade and investment, will be of decisive importance in impelling the governments of Egypt and Israel toward a settlement of their political differences. However, both parties are committed to the peace process, and they realize that economic relations are an important tangible demonstration of their political intentions toward each other. Thus, both countries publicly support normalization, of which economic relations are an important component.

Egypt and Israel have conflicting views about the desired volume of bilateral transactions in the near future, a clash that ought to be recognized and understood at the outset. Israel wishes, for political reasons, to expand the scope of economic relations, whereas Egypt is interested in minimizing it. Israel's attitude is easily understood, for the peace agreement obliged Israel to return to Egyptian territories that have considerable strategic and economic importance. The Sinai Peninsula contains oil and other minerals and, in recent years, had become a source of tourist income. More important still was its military significance, because it provided Israel with an irreplaceable strategic hinterland. All these real assets were surrendered in return for the peace agreement, which—although tremendously significant—is only a declaration of intent. From Israel's point of view, economic transactions such as trade, investments, and movement of people, goods, and services, provide the concrete contents of the peace. Without such flows peace remains an empty and fragile shell that can easily be broken.

The Egyptians have a different point of view. By making peace with Israel they have granted it something it had been denied since its establishment: formal recognition by its greatest adversary, which had taken a leading role in all the Arab-Israeli wars. In return, so argue the Egyptians, Israel has given back to Egypt territories that had been Egyptian in the first place. The Palestinian question, which has always been and still remains the core of the Arab-Israeli conflict, remains unsolved. Establishment of friendly relations between Egypt and Israel, of which close economic relations are but one aspect, must be preceded by a settlement of the Lebanon issue and by noticeable progress on the Palestinian question, according to the Egyptian view.

Actual economic relations between Egypt and Israel are fashioned by policies representing a compromise between these conflicting views. The compromise, however, inevitably favors the Egyptian view. This is because whenever two parties disagree on the volume of bilateral transactions between them, the party that seeks to minimize the volume is, of course, usually in a more powerful position. It is difficult to force this party to buy or sell more than it wishes, so it is the Egyptians who decide on the upper bounds of the volume of transactions with Israel. The Israelis or third parties must persuade them that it is in their interest to increase the scope and volume of economic transactions if trade is to expand.

Partial success in this direction is represented by the Egyptian-Israeli oil agreement incorporated into the economic provisions of the peace treaty. It provides a clear example of a politically motivated transaction that could have a profound effect on future economic relations between the two countries. The oil agreement negotiated in 1979 provided for the sale of substantial quantities of oil by Egypt to Israel, ostensibly to replace the oil that Israel had previously pumped from the oil wells it held and partially developed in the Sinai. The agreement's significance from Israel's point of view lay at least partly in the fact that it obliged Egypt to publicly enter into a long-term agreement with the former enemy. Economically, the agreement is not of great significance because there is a ready world market for oil and because the transactions are based on world market prices. Nevertheless, the oil agreement has benefited both countries: it provides Egypt with a reliable market and Israel with a steady and close supplier. Both sides presumably share the savings in transport costs in an equitable manner.

While the oil agreement between Egypt and Israel appears to be satisfactory per se, it leads to a substantial deficit in Israel's current account with Egypt, since trade in other goods and services has been quite small. This imbalance in Israel's bilateral current account might be at least partially corrected by adopting the compensation principle, that is, by enabling Israel to pay for all or part of the oil with goods and services rather than with convertible currency. Barter, as is well known, is not a very efficient way of distributing the gains from international exchange, but it is quite common, especially when politically sensitive transactions are involved. Moreover, Egypt has barter arrangements in many of its international transactions, especially with countries of the Eastern bloc. If the principle of trading oil against goods were accepted, two-way trade between Egypt and Israel could reach several hundred million dollars in a short time. In the absence of such an arrangement, the Egyptian-Israeli trade balance is likely to remain in favor of the former for some years to come.

LONG-TERM CONSIDERATIONS

Political considerations will undoubtedly continue to influence Egyptian-Israeli economic relations even after the immediate political difficulties are resolved. Two concepts ought to influence the political economy of these relations in the long term: vested interest in peace and optimal interdependence.

The first term refers to the effect of bilateral economic transactions between recent belligerents on the attitude of the populations in question toward peace. We assume that attitude toward peace, like attitude toward other questions of national concern, is influenced to some degree by the effect of policies under consideration on the economic welfare of the persons or groups whose attitude is being considered. Thus, if peace can be shown to improve the economic well-being of a certain group, support for peace in this group is expected to rise. Conversely, peace is expected to enjoy less support among groups that are adversely affected by its consequences. Vested interest in peace is, according to this view, directly related to changes in material welfare that can be attributed to peace.

This definition of vested interest in peace and the description of factors determining it may appear to be overly pessimistic. This approach apparently suggests that people's views are formed in response to their immediate and short-term material interest; even their economic calculations are extremely myopic, because they ignore the benefits from the reduction in defense burden that peace ultimately makes possible.

This is not necessarily the case. Public attitude toward peace is obviously influenced by political, psychological, ideological, as well as economic, factors. [1] Peace may be fragile not because it conflicts with narrow economic interests within the countries concerned, but because of genuine political differences and the difficulties in finding compromises among conflicting claims.

International trade theory shows that, under most circumstances, voluntarily assumed international transactions are profitable. Overall and even individual welfare can be increased, since the extra real income made available by the exchange could be distributed among the citizens of the country in question. There is, however, no automatic mechanism ensuring such redistribution, and thus it may be that while some individuals gain, others lose. The effect of international transactions on vested interest in peace is, therefore, indeterminate unless steps are taken to compensate those whose welfare is adversely affected or to impose restrictions on international transactions. In the second case, only transactions whose overall economic benefits are clearly discernible and that cause no economic injury to politically articulate sections of the population will be allowed.

As long as peace is fragile, it makes sense to promote economic and noneconomic activities that will increase support for the peace process by demonstrating its benefits. It makes equally good sense to refrain from promoting activities that make peace seem less palatable economically. Thus, we assume that both governments will seek to adopt policies intended to promote vested interest in peace within their jurisdictions. Bearing in mind that not all bilateral economic transactions are necessarily consistent with this principle, it may be desirable to set up mechanisms to monitor specific trade and investment flows between Egyptian and Israeli enterprises, to assess their impact on vested interest in peace in each country, to encourage transactions likely to promote it, and to discourage or modify transactions that may adversely affect it. If these policies are to be successful, some method of consultation, and possibly of coordination, should be adopted between the two countries.

Optimal interdependence refers to the effect of bilateral transactions on the power relationship between the countries under consideration. Trade and other economic transactions have been shown to increase the welfare of the parties undertaking them. Simultaneously, however, bilateral transactions create mutual dependence.

Dependence, if not carefully watched, can be asymmetric and can lead to abuses. To understand how dependence occurs, I introduce the concept of "cost of dissociation." This is the cost incurred by parties engaged in economic transactions when the transactions are discontinued. When two parties agree to transact they presumably expect to benefit from the transaction. If the transactions are discontinued, the expected benefits fail to materialize. The cost of dissociation, then, is equal to the benefits that are forgone owing to discontinuation of the planned transactions.

The relationship between cost of dissociation and dependence is straightforward. Assume that costs of dissociation are substantial and one-sided. In that case, if country A can, by dissociating, inflict substantial hardships on country B, and country B is unable to retaliate, then country B is said to be dependent on country A. Country A could use its superior bargaining power to exact either political or economic concessions from country B.

Cost of dissociation need not be proportional to the volume of bilateral trade, to its relative importance, or to the essentiality of the goods traded. To illustrate this point, consider once again the Egyptian-Israeli oil agreement. Both countries gain from the transaction—Egypt, having a surplus of oil, gains scarce dollars; Israel, having no indigenous oil, has a convenient source of supply. Now consider the effect of dissociation—the nullification of the agreement. The effect will be very small, because Egypt can sell its oil elsewhere, probably at prices not much lower than the price it can obtain from Israel. Israel, too, has alternative sources of supply that are unlikely to be more expensive. Thus, even if Israel were to obtain a high proportion of its oil from Egypt and even if Egypt were to sell a high proportion of its oil to Israel, the cost of dissociation would be small as long as the transactions between them were at world market prices, and as long as Egypt has alternative markets and Israel has alternative sources of supply.

Consider, however, another example. Assume that Egypt and Israel agree to build jointly a number of nuclear power stations designed to serve both countries. If a substantial share of electricity used in both countries were to come from such joint projects, then the cost of dissociation would be high.

Note that the cost is high not because atomic energy is necessarily chearper than other forms of energy. The cost is high because power generation is not an instantaneous process. It takes years to build a power plant, and once a decision to generate power by a certain method is implemented, this decision can be revoked only at a

very high cost during the lifetime of the plant. Thus, the world depends on oil not solely because oil is (or was) so much cheaper than,
say, coal. It depends on oil also, or perhaps primarily, because of
the long time lag and enormous resources required to convert from
oil to alternative fuels. The cost of dissociating from oil thus includes the outlay on complementary investments in power-generating
capacity and in other energy-using installations. It also includes the
loss of output attributable to the shortage of power until alternative
sources of energy are both located and made available.

Professor A. O. Hirschman of Princeton University's Institute
for Advanced Study has shown in a penetrating study of Germany's
prewar international economic policies how Nazi Germany deliberately
used the notion of cost of dissociation to achieve political domination
over the Balkan states during the 1930s.[2] Germany offered these
countries access to its own highly protected markets on privileged
terms and sold them various goods at prices representing substantial
discounts from world market prices. Gradually, more and more economic sectors in those countries became dependent on the German
market or the German supplies. Dissociation for them would have
brought economic ruin. The governments of these countries soon
realized that unless they supported Germany politically, they would
suffer considerable economic losses. The threat of dissociation was
thus transformed into political domination, or one-way dependence.[3]

One-way dependence, however, is not the only possible outcome
of economic relations between two countries. Bilateral transactions
can lead to mutual dependence or interdependence. Dependence is
mutual, or symmetrical, when the cost of dissociation is balanced,
in the sense that dissociation for one country is more or less as pain-
ful as it is for the other.

When properly planned and executed, interdependence enables
gains from bilateral transactions and losses from dissociation to be
both substantial and symmetrical. Thus, when one party decides to
dissociate, its own expected losses and those of the other party are
of a similar order of magnitude. When a reasonable balance is a
achieved between both parties' costs of dissociation, they are considered to be optimally interdependent.

Interdependence between any two countries, let alone between
recent belligerents, is difficult to plan and control. This is partly because of the complex way in which individual transactions, often decided by businessmen interested in making profits, add to the cost of
dissociation if and when it occurs. Thus, there may well be divergence
between private and public interests. Public interest is not necessarily
to prevent the cost of dissociation from exceeding a certain level; it
is to prevent relative costs of dissociation from changing in a direc-

tion that will alter the relationship from interdependence to one-way dependence. Since each transaction adds to the costs of dissociation of both countries, monitoring and control become rather complicated.

Only rarely do the incremental decisions of individual businesses lead to an asymmetrical buildup of one country's cost of dissociation. Therefore, it is common under normal circumstances for market economies to entrust a high proportion of their international transactions to individual firms. However, even market economies adopt special policies regarding so-called strategic materials, and their governments tend to intervene in transactions involving nonmarket economies whose trade and other economic transactions are highly centralized and are often motivated by political considerations. It is only sensible to add to this list transactions between recent or, for that matter, potential belligerents.

The common denominator in all these cases is the cost of dissociation. This cost can be rightly ignored when alternative suppliers or markets exist, or when political and economic relations between trading partners make dissociation unthinkable. When dissociation is a distinct possibility, the government has a legitimate concern with the volume, composition, and terms of the transactions with the country in question.

Recent belligerents seeking to stabilize a fragile peace cannot afford to ignore these factors. If they do, they may find that their economic relations lead to instability, creating conflict and damage rather than enhancing the economic vested interest in peace that properly handled bilateral transactions can promote.

EGYPTIAN-ISRAELI ECONOMIC COOPERATION

As was noted earlier in this chapter, considerations pertaining to enhancement of vested interest in peace and to attainment of optimal interdependence should influence the volume, composition, and direction of trends, investment, and other economic transactions between Egypt and Israel, even after the political difficulties currently hampering development of bilateral economic relations are resolved.

Despite the centrality of political considerations, it is important to analyze the potential for trade and other transactions between the countries from a purely economic point of view, especially since this potential is not a given quantity waiting to be discovered and exploited like a natural resource or a physical entity. The potential is determined by numerous factors, some of which may in turn be influenced by policy decisions. Realization of this potential will require planning, allocation of resources, and time. Consequently, it makes sense to examine the nature, volume, and composition of potential economic transactions between Egypt and Israel, despite the uncertainties about political conditions and the institutional framework of these transactions.

Egypt and Israel can enjoy substantial gains from bilateral economic transactions involving trade, investment, and transfer of technology. These benefits are predicated on the proximity factor, which allows producers in one country to service consumers in the other while enjoying cost advantages in transportation, marketing, communication, and servicing over the more distant competitors from Europe, the United States, or Japan. Added to the proximity factor are resource complementarities. Labor, capital, raw materials of different kinds, know-how, marketing connections, and other resources from one country can, when combined with resources from the other, improve the competitive position of both economies in domestic markets as well as in third-country markets. These factors may in turn be coupled with economies of scale, thereby reducing unit costs by expanding output to a more economical level. At times, the potential for economies of scale cannot be exploited owing to the smallness of the domestic market. When nearby markets or sources of supply are made accessible by the establishment of normal economic relations— as in the case of Egypt and Israel—utilization of economies of scale becomes feasible.

This analysis yields certain clues regarding the economic and technological characteristics of candidates for bilateral trade between past belligerents. Such candidates will tend to have relatively high transfer costs. Perishables such as fresh fruit, vegetables, meat, milk, and milk products immediately come to mind. Cement, quarry products, and building materials are other candidates. The list of potential candidates is not exhausted, however, by bulky, low-cost products of the kind just mentioned. Transfer costs, in addition to transportation costs, also consist of outlays on marketing and provision of services. Proximity to the market can undoubtedly help reduce service costs of appliances, computer installations, industrial equipment, and even provision of services such as medicine, planning, design, insurance, and banking. These activities might figure prominently in the exchange between neighboring countries such as Egypt and Israel.

The production of some goods that might be candidates for bilateral trade between the two countries is likely to be characterized by economies of scale. On their own, economies of scale are of little importance in the present context. When manufacture of a product is characterized by negative correlation between volume of output and unit costs, small size of the domestic market need not prevent the product from being internationally competitive. Only when transfer costs are substantial may the small size of the domestic market prove to be a decisive obstacle. In this case, the opening of a neighboring market may be of crucial importance.

Potential gains from economic intercourse between recent belligerents are not exhausted by trade in goods and services. Additional gains are offered by establishing cooperative ventures that combine production factors from the two countries and that enable the joint enterprises to compete internationally in cases where single-country enterprises cannot. Such ventures may, in certain cases, compete with imports from third countries. In other cases they may enable the recent belligerents to export jointly goods and services that they would have to import individually if they failed to pool their resources.

Cooperative ventures need not be limited to two parties, but can be based on three or more. The addition of third parties increases the list of potentially competitive ventures and total gains from cooperation. Moreover, third-party involvement may be viewed by the past belligerents as a partial insurance against the other side deciding to dissociate. It therefore reduces the risk of dissociation and further increases the scope for cooperation between recent belligerents.

Proximity, combined with resource complementarities and economies of scale, can lead to a substantial expansion of the two countries' tradeable sector—that is, the sector producing goods and services that are traded internationally.

Such an expansion of the tradeable sector requires, as was noted above, long-term commitment of capital, managerial, and other resources that are particularly scarce in Egypt. Israeli firms seeking to do business in Egypt, therefore, are often required to accompany the sale of goods with transfer of know-how and provision of services, credit, and even long-term capital. Investment-related trade is thus likely to figure prominently in Egyptian-Israeli economic transactions.

The potential for investment-related trade between Egypt and Israel is further enhanced by recent developments in the Egyptian economy. Egypt's gross national product (GNP) has been expanding at a high rate since the late 1970s. Expansion has been accompanied, and to some extent facilitated, by a substantial increase in foreign exchange inflows from oil, tourism, Suez Canal fees, workers' remittances from abroad, and foreign aid. These flows, which by 1980 had reached about $10,000 million, reduced but did not eliminate Egypt's current balance deficit. They more than made up for the loss of income caused by withdrawal of Arab aid in retaliation for Egypt's decision to make peace with Israel.

The increase in income, however, was not fully matched by expansion of productive capacity. Consequently, Egypt's economic

growth has been constrained by bottlenecks in the country's infrastructure, public services, and productive capacity in a growing number
of sectors, as well as by a continuing shortage of foreign exchange.

The supply bottlenecks characterizing the Egyptian economy affect not only the country's import-substituting industries, but also
its actual and potential exportables. In the short term, Egypt simply
does not have the productive capacity to take care of domestic requirements, let alone exports. Thus, Egypt imports goods and services
that clearly promote a long-term comparative advantage. Egypt is
a net importer of many fruits, vegetables, and dairy products; cement,
iron, and steel; textiles and clothing; and numerous other goods that,
potentially, could be domestically produced on a competitive basis
once productive capacity is sufficiently expanded.

The Egyptian government has been anxious to reduce the country's import dependence by relieving some of the bottlenecks described above. To achieve this goal, the government has given high
priority to investments in construction, industry, and agriculture.
Business firms, including foreign firms, are encouraged to participate
in this endeavor through tax concessions, liberal import rules, and
other regulations regarding transfer of earnings, subsidized loans,
and other incentives.

Thus, firms wishing to do business with Egypt are likely to find
that by combining trade with investment or trade with the provision
of needed technological and managerial know-how, they will encounter
a more ready market than firms limiting themselves to trade alone.

The following case studies illustrate the concepts of combining
trade with investment or with technological and managerial expertise,
which may become the major vehicle of Egyptian-Israeli economic
cooperation in the long term. [4]

THREE CASE STUDIES

The Textile and Clothing Industry

Textile and clothing industries are found in most countries, regardless of their stage of development. They account for a significant
percentage of the value added and employment even in the United
States (6 percent and 11 percent, respectively), while in several developing countries the share of value added and employment may exceed one-third.

In recent years a decline in these industries (at least in some
of their more labor-intensive operations) has occurred in the industrialized countries, and a corresponding increase has occurred in the
developing countries.

Egypt's textile and clothing industry employed approximately 350,000 workers in 1980 and has been that country's leading industry, accounting for 30 percent of industrial employment. Over two-thirds of the industry's output comes from spinning and weaving, mostly (about 80 percent) by state-owned enterprises. Clothing and wearing apparel, representing the balance, have been growing at a more rapid rate. The private-sector share in this segment of the industry has been quite high, reaching about 60 percent.

The industry's major export has been textile yarn and thread, but cotton cloth and fabric have been quite important also, reaching approximately 20 percent of total exports of nearly $300 million in 1979. Despite Egypt's comparative advantage in the labor-intensive clothing and wearing apparel sector, only about 10 percent of the industry's exports and about 6 percent of its output come from this sector. In addition, nearly $400 million of raw cotton, mainly the long-staple variety, was exported in 1979.

Israel's textile and clothing industry, which is mostly in the private sector, employs approximately 50,000 workers and accounts for 18 percent of industrial employment. It has a gross output of about $1,200 million, of which roughly 37 percent or $450 million was exported in 1980 mainly to Western markets. Of this, nearly two-thirds was in clothing and ready-made articles.

In recent years, the industry's share in value added of the manufacturing sector has declined, although it has grown in absolute terms. Among the different subsectors, yarn and cloth have been declining, while clothing has been growing at an impressive rate. Israel is also a cotton-growing country (mainly medium-staple cotton), with exports in 1980 reaching $100 million.

The industries of Egypt and Israel are characterized by a fair degree of complementarity that could help create a mutually beneficial division of labor. Egypt could supply Israel with cotton yarn and cloth; Israel could reciprocate with synthetics. Israel could import Egyptian long-staple cotton and Egypt could import the short-staple variety. Egypt utilizes much of its long-staple cotton to produce inexpensive clothing and charges industry much less than the export price. If priced at export value, then real value added on clothing may be negative. Cotton countertrade with Israel might change this situation to both countries' mutual benefit.

The most interesting potential for cooperation, however, lies in the clothing industry. In this case both countries could learn a great deal from Western European industry, which managed to survive despite fierce competition from both within and outside Europe. It did so by breaking down the production process into several stages and by performing each stage in locations with competitive advantages vis-à-vis the rest of the world.

As was noted above, Israel's clothing industry has a strong export orientation. Over the years it has established a reasonably strong market position in Western Europe and, to a lesser degree, in the United States. Israel's position in Western European markets has been buttressed by its agreement with the European Economic Community (EEC). This agreement guarantees access to most of Israel's manufacturers on terms equal to those of domestic European manufacturers. Further expansion of exports from Israel appears to be hampered by supply bottlenecks, especially shortage of labor.

Cooperation with Egypt could alleviate some of these shortages. Because Egypt has an obvious advantage in labor-intensive operations such as sewing, Israeli and Egyptian firms could cooperate either by subcontracting or by establishing joint ventures. Egyptian firms could in turn take advantage of Israel's capabilities in design, printing, dyeing, and finishing. Geographic proximity is of great importance in this context because it facilitates communication and physical shipment of goods at short notice.

In the longer run, the more dominant method of cooperation will probably entail firms from one country engaging in direct investments in the other, setting up subsidiaries that are integrated with the parent. This form of business has advantages over more relaxed forms of cooperation because it facilitates closer coordination and more efficient utilization of centralized functions such as marketing, design, and quality control.

Establishment of manufacturing operations that draw on the competitive advantages of Egypt (cotton, yarn and cloth production, sewing and other labor-intensive processes) and Israel (design, printing, and finishing) may be attractive not only to Egyptian and Israeli firms. Firms from the EEC that have preferential trade agreements with both Egypt and Israel may be able to take advantage of potentially competitive new sources of supply. Firms from countries such as the United States or Japan, which have no free-trade agreement with the EEC, may also wish to capitalize on the opportunities offered by combining the advantages of Egypt and Israel.

Full-scale utilization of potential advantages in Egyptian-Israeli cooperation in the textile and clothing industries will require modifications in rules, regulations, and other agreements concerning industry in the two countries. A suitable institutional framework may be based on the model of the European Coal and Steel Community, which preceded the establishment of the EEC and which was built on a wide-ranging sectorial, not comprehensive, integration covering the entire economies of the countries involved.

The textile and clothing industries in Egypt and Israel exhibit such a wide range of potential complementarities that cooperation between them may yield substantial dividends in the form of a strong competitive position in existing and new markets, as well as in existing and new lines of business. It could indeed make sense for both governments to promote cooperation by making suitable institutional arrangements to facilitate movement of goods, services, capital, and know-how between enterprises in the textile and clothing industries. Such a policy is bound to improve the competitive position and export performance of the industries in both countries. It is also likely to facilitate increased investment from both domestic and foreign enterprises.

The Fertilizer Industry

Of the three primary fertilizer ingredients, nitrogen (N), phosphorus (P, P_2O_5, phosphate), and potassium (K, K_2O, potash), Egypt possesses the mineral resources needed to manufacture nitrogen and phosphate fertilizers, and Israel has the mineral resources to manufacture phosphate and potash fertilizers. Jointly, the two countries can provide all three ingredients, and this may give them a competitive advantage in the international fertilizer markets.

In 1980 Israel's 2 million ton net output represented nearly 2 percent of the world's NPK output and over 4 percent of world NPK trade. The industry is dominated by the state-owned Israel Chemicals Limited (ICL), which controls over 80 percent of output, employment, and exports and accounts for over two-thirds of output alone. The ICL is further expanding its capacity of downstream products for international marketing, but the industry depends on imported ammonia based on oil or gas.

Egypt's fertilizer industry has developed more slowly than Israel's. In 1980 it produced about 0.5 percent and consumed about 0.6 percent of world NPK output. However, Egypt is soon expected to achieve self-sufficiency at approximately 750,000 tons. Nevertheless, owing to a shortage of specific items and surpluses in others, imports may still be required, especially to supply the growing need for potash.

Having lost the fertilizing effect of the Nile waters, Egypt is developing an ever-growing need for chemical fertilizers. Availability of a compound NPK fertilizer would simplify the application of all three elements by a farming sector not easily guided by economic incentives.

A complex located in Egypt to produce NPK fertilizers based on an ammonia unit of some 500,000 tons per year, drawing its potash requirements from Israel and its phosphoric acid from both Israel and

Egypt, could fulfill Egypt's NPK needs during the 1980s. The complementary requirements for PK or NP combinations could be supplemented from existing facilities in Israel until such time as the volume grew to justify establishment of Egyptian-based production units of PK and NP. The ammonia unit could supply some 20 percent of its output to Israel in exchange for the potash and phosphoric acid.

While the project is being evaluated, planned, and constructed, an extraregional industrial partner could assist the commercial development by supplying Israel with ammonia and by taking phosphoric acid, potash, and granulated P and PK fertilizers in exchange from the ICL companies. The presence of a third-country partner would ensure security of supply in case political or technical difficulties arise. The contribution of an international fertilizer firm could augment the existing advantages and could provide additional capital, expertise, marketing networks, and mediation services.

The project could be substantially expanded if the parties decided to jointly develop a production mechanism for export of NPK products.

To conclude, cooperation between Egypt and Israel in the fertilizer industry could yield substantial dividends. It could strengthen the competitive position and export performance of both countries. Although initial cooperation might be limited to an agreement between Egyptian and Israeli companies, it could possibly evolve into cooperative ventures with third-country parties. Institutional arrangements facilitating movement of goods, processes, capital, and know-how in this sector would further enhance cooperative projects. In addition, a policy of cooperation is likely to promote increased investments from both domestic and foreign enterprises.

The Cement Industry

Cement is a bulky product whose value relative to its weight is low. Consequently, it is not usually transported over long distances. The production process is subject to significant economies of scale, and the minimum size of an efficient plant is large. When a new plant is built, the addition to a small country's production capacity can be quite substantial. Thus, temporary excess capacity is often found in a country or region where a new plant has been recently completed. Because the production process is highly capital-intensive and marginal costs are low, it pays to produce at full capacity and to export the surplus as long as prices exceed marginal costs. This alternative is preferable to production at less than full capacity, which raises unit costs substantially. Exports are only temporary as a rule, since capacity is designed to take care of normal domestic demand. As domestic demand expands, exports are first reduced and finally discontinued. If and when domestic demand expands further, temporary imports are required to take care of it, because expansion implies a substantial increase in capacity that cannot be effected at short notice.

The timing and volume of new investments create a tricky situation, particularly in small countries, because of the bulkiness of the investment. Thus, small countries are likely to depend more on foreign trade in cement than are large countries. Such dependence is undesirable because of the high cost of transportation coupled with substantial uncertainties over supplies, markets, and prices.

Cooperation between Egypt and Israel in the cement industry could benefit both countries in several respects. If trade barriers to cement are eliminated, the two countries can form a single market, thus benefiting from economies of scale and depending less on erratic markets and suppliers.

As of the end of 1980, both Egypt (with six plants) and Israel (with three) have been short of cement and both countries have been planning to increase their production capacity over the coming years. Establishment of economic relations between the two countries raises some interesting questions regarding the location of Israel's fourth plant. The plant could conceivably be located in Egypt, since Egypt enjoys a considerable cost advantage in energy, which used intensively in the manufacture of cement. Cost savings in energy could compensate for the higher transportation costs of shipping cement over long distances. Tentative calculations indicate that a plant located in Egypt could compete with one in Israel in the Israeli market if the former could obtain gas at a price representing a 30 percent to 35 percent discount over the cost of energy obtained from coal imported by Israel. A transaction of this kind could be profitable for Egypt, considering the alternative uses for its gas.

Assuming that this transaction does occur, let us see how some of the concepts developed earlier can give additional insights into the project's possible effects on both countries.

Peaceful relations with Israel make it possible to establish in Egypt a potentially welfare-enhancing new export industry that will earn urgently needed foreign exchange. If prices are competitive, consumer welfare in Israel, too, will be raised. However, other factors must be examined as well. Consider the nature and extent of mutual dependence generated by the project. Egyptian plants, each employing over one hundred people, become dependent on a single foreign market. Bearing in mind the high transportation costs, it is unlikely that alternative export markets will be as profitable. The

Israelis depend on a single foreign supplier for about one-quarter of their cement, which is an important material in the construction industry. If supplies are discontinued, alternative sources are bound to be more expensive. Both sides should consider additional risks: If Egyptian domestic demand rises, will prices be raised or supplies diverted? If demand in Israel slackens, will the Israelis reduce domestic purchases, or will they reduce their imports instead?

Questions such as these inevitably surface whenever bulky investment projects are considered. In the present context, however, it is not only the economic welfare of those affected by the decision that is at stake; the peace process, too, may be affected. This is so because, for each country, it is the recent enemy that will appear responsible for both the gains from cooperation and the losses caused by disruption. Clearly, no government can be indifferent to either possibility. For this reason, governments must play an important role in establishing rules governing the volume and form of bilateral transactions between recent belligerents.

CONCLUDING REMARKS

The projects discussed in the previous sections have several common characteristics that make them suitable for enhancing the peace process. They fit in with the national priorities of both countries by generating much-needed foreign exchange earnings through export expansion (fertilizers, textiles, and clothing for both countries, and cement for Egypt alone). More important in the present context, the projects conform to the criteria of enhancing vested interest in peace and interdependence. They have the potential to generate new jobs and additional sources of income without adversely affecting existing economic activities. Their realization enhances interdependence in another sense, because they cannot exist without bilateral cooperation between the two countries. Since their economic rationale is based on complementarities, cooperation makes it possible to effectively combine inputs from the two countries in a manner enhancing the international competitiveness of both. By the same token, if cooperation is discontinued, both parties stand to lose.

A final point: Egypt and Israel develop their economic relations from a zero base. Each economic transaction, especially those accompanied by long-term commitments of funds and other resources, will simultaneously affect welfare and cost of dissociation in both countries. Each transaction can therefore be regarded as having some political implications that are of legitimate concern to both governments.

It is not too early to think of unilateral and bilateral institutional arrangements that will be explicitly charged with promoting vested interest in peace and interdependence, and with devising policies and mechanisms to help both governments decide on a level and composition of bilateral economic transactions that will be compatible with their national interests, while at the same time enhancing the peace process.

NOTES

1. For a detailed discussion of the relationship between economic factors and attitudes toward war in Europe, see Raymond Aron, The Century of Total War (Boston: Beacon Press, 1966), chap. 3.

2. Albert O. Hirschman, National Power and the Structure of Foreign Trade (Berkeley and Los Angeles: University of California Press, 1969).

3. Ibid., p. 29.

4. Based on reports prepared by Simha Bahiri for the Tel Aviv University Project for Joint Economic Development in the Middle East. The cement industry case was previously published in R. Arad and Z. Hirsch, "Peacemaking and Vested Interests," International Studies Quarterly 25, no. 3 (September 1981): 465-67.

7

MIDDLE EAST DEVELOPMENT
FUNDS AND BANKS:
AN OVERVIEW

SHIREEN T. HUNTER

INTRODUCTION

During the last decade, the Middle East has undergone tremendous social, political, and economic change. From a political perspective, a number of countries that only a decade ago remained largely on the periphery of regional politics—notably the states of the Persian Gulf—have become central players both regionally and internationally. At the same time, two important Middle East countries, Egypt and Israel, demonstrated great political courage and foresight in starting a process that, if continued to its distant conclusion, could bring a far greater measure of peace and stability to the area. Unfortunately, however, the danger of armed conflict has been recently demonstrated in Lebanon and continues in other parts of the Middle East (as in the case of the Iran-Iraq war) and on the region's periphery (as in the Horn of Africa, North Africa, and sub-Saharan Africa).

From an economic perspective, the region as a whole has registered a considerable growth rate with the inflow of vast amounts of oil income, although differences in the level of economic development and in the standard of living among individual countries remain high. Moreover, together with this rapid economic growth and the development of potentially significant industrial centers, economic relations within the region have also expanded. For example, there has been increased mobility of labor and capital, and a considerable degree of regional cooperation has taken place on economic and financial matters. There has also been a significant increase in the number of joint industrial and trade ventures in the region. The effect of recent declines in oil prices will undoubtedly affect these developments, although the nature of these effects is not clear.

The impact of economic development has not been limited to regional relations. For example, political and economic interaction between Middle East and other developing countries has increased. The presence of large numbers of skilled and unskilled workers from the Indian subcontinent, Turkey, Southeast Asia, and even certain African countries (for example, the Sudan) is a graphic illustration of this new situation. One estimate[1] puts the number of nonindigenous workers in the Persian Gulf as follows:

Gulf Countries	Active Expatriates (in thousands)	Percentage of Working Population
Saudi Arabia	1,300	56.5
Bahrain	30	50.0
United Arab Emirates	239	80.0
Kuwait	211	71.0
Qatar	54	81.0
Oman	70	20.0

Yet another facet of this new situation has been the involvement of developing countries in construction and other aspects of the region's economic development. Firms from South Korea, Taiwan, the Philippines, India, and Turkey are doing considerable business in the area. According to one source, for example, 53 Turkish firms are working on construction projects in the Middle East valued at an estimated $2,943 million.[2]

Relations with industrialized countries have also not been exempt from the impact of the new economic situation in the Middle East. In fact, Middle East interaction and interdependence with industrial nations have reached unprecedented levels. For example, fully 13 percent of the total external trade of the European Economic Community (EEC) is now with the Arab states of the Middle East, and these countries have replaced the United States (at 11 percent) as the EEC's first trading partner.

Unfortunately, not all these economic changes have been positive, particularly from the point of view of the oil exporters. For example, rapid economic development has strained the traditional sociopolitical fabric of Middle East societies. It has also taxed the capacity of existing political and economic institutions to adjust to constantly

evolving situations, as well as their capacity to channel newly un-
leashed energies into constructive activities. In Iran's case, changes
were so rapid and their effects so destabilizing that they resulted in
revolution and total collapse of the political system. Clearly, no
country in the Middle East is totally immune to the destabilizing effects of change.

Moreover, in view of the increased level of interaction between
the Middle East and other countries, the impact of negative developments, as Iran's case clearly demonstrates, can no longer be limited
to one country or even to one region.

Yet, on balance, the last decade has been a time of increased
social and political growth and maturity for the region. A sign of this
emerging maturity has been the increasing awareness, shown by those
Middle East countries that have gained in power and status, of responsibilities deriving from their new position as active and influential
members of both the regional and international communities. Whether
they have always succeeded in recognizing correctly the practical implications of these new responsibilities, or have discharged them effectively, is another matter. But the awareness clearly exists.

These newly acquired responsibilities have several dimensions,
with that of economics being particularly important. The economic
dimension includes a variety of factors, ranging from some sharing
of responsibility with industrial states for maintenance (and even a
bit of management) of international economic and financial stability,
to a need to contribute to development financing within both the Middle
East and the rest of the developing world. Again, whether the performance of these countries has been up to regional and international
expectations is debatable, but the fact remains that their efforts and
contributions have by any standard been quite substantial. See Table
7.1 for figures on official development assistance by Organization of
Petroleum Exporting Countries (OPEC) member countries during the
period 1973-79.

One consequence of the increased involvement of oil-rich Middle
East countries in development financing has been the establishment of
several development funds and banks in the region—although the idea
and even the creation of one development fund, the Kuwait Fund for
Arab Economic Development (KFAED), predates recent events. (Of
course, development banks and funds are only one aspect of assistance
programs by Middle East countries, which also extend aid through international channels and through a variety of bilateral arrangements.)

Despite considerable economic progress, however, Middle East
development needs remain enormous. Ideally, a consolidation of
existing Middle East development institutions, and some changes in
their methods of operations, would best serve the interests of the re-

TABLE 7.1

Development Assistance by OPEC Member Countries,
Official Net Disbursements, 1973-79

Year	Amount (in millions of dollars)	Percentage of Gross National Product
1973	1,308	1.42
1974	3,447	1.96
1975	5,517	2.94
1976	5,593	2.43
1977	5,858	2.12
1978	4,338	1.38
1979	5,197	1.44

Note: This excludes Ecuador, Gabon, and Indonesia.

gion. But in view of the near impossibility of such a development in the foreseeable future, an argument can be made that there should be at least one new institution instead, particularly one able to bring more imagination and creativity to solving regional economic problems. For such a new institution to succeed and to gain regional acceptance, it must not appear to duplicate or compete with existing institutions. In addition, other requirements, if met, could increase the chances of success for such an institution.

This chapter identifies the most important of these requirements by reviewing the background, structure, objectives, development philosophy, and performance record of the existing funds and banks. This chapter is not, however, about OPEC aid or even Middle East aid in its totality. Rather, it deals with one aspect of this new phenomenon, namely, Middle East development institutions.

The idea of establishing some kind of economic development institution for the Middle East was first aired within the context of the Arab League during the 1950s. But a variety of problems, including lack of sufficient financial resources, delayed its creation. Only in 1968 was basic agreement reached on the establishment of an Arab Fund for Economic and Social Development (AFESD), based on a plan largely developed by Kuwait, and the fund did not become operational until 1972.

The AFESD was the first regional development fund in the Middle East, but it was not the area's first nationally based fund. In fact, by 1972 Kuwait and the United Arab Emirates had already set up their own national development funds to assist the development efforts of

Arab states and, later, of other developing countries. Kuwait was the pioneer, setting up its fund shortly after independence in 1961. Its experience was quite successful, and this success later helped prompt other Middle East countries to follow suit. Moreover, the Kuwaitis actively encouraged others to do so.

TYPES OF DEVELOPMENT FUNDS

The Middle East development funds fall into two broad categories: national and regional.

National funds include the Kuwait Fund for Arab Economic Development, the Abu Dhabi Fund for Arab Economic Development (ADFAED), the Saudi Development Fund, and the Iraqi Fund for External Development. Two other Middle East countries—Iran and Libya—have been involved in development assistance, but do not have a development fund. Iran's assistance program was largely handled by the Organization for Investment, Economic, and Technical Assistance; and Libya's by the Libyan Arab Foreign Bank.

The area has only one regional fund, the Arab Fund for Economic and Social Development. On the basis of membership, source of capital, and scope of operations, this is the only truly regional fund in the Middle East.

Two other institutions exist outside these categories, but because of either the composition of their membership or sources of capital, they nevertheless have very close links with the Middle East: the Islamic Development Bank (IsDB) and the Arab Bank for Economic Development in Africa (BADEA). Despite the fact that capital for BADEA is provided by the Arab countries of the Middle East, it is principally an African institution, since its beneficiaries are solely non-Arab African states. The IsDB case is less clear, but given the concentration of Muslim countries in the Middle East—especially if the region is defined in broad geographical terms—the IsDB could be considered to be a Middle East regional bank with transregional dimensions.

Assistance from OPEC member countries, in contrast, does not properly constitute a Middle East regional fund, although the bulk of such capital is provided by countries from that area, because of OPEC's international character and the global ambitions of its fund. See Tables 7.2 and 7.3 for the authorized and paid-in capital of these and other OPEC-related organizations. Assistance is also given by the Arab Monetary Fund (AMF) to Arab countries, and by the Islamic Solidarity Fund (ISF) to Muslim communities in non-Islamic countries. The ISF is managed by the IsDB.

TABLE 7.2

Authorized Capital of OPEC Aid Institutions
(in millions of dollars)

Institution	Authorized Capital
Islamic Solidarity Fund	113
Abu Dhabi Fund for Arab Economic Development	541
Arab Authority for Agricultural Investment and Development	562
Iraqi Fund for External Development	677
Arab Bank for Economic Development in Africa	738
Arab Monetary Fund	1,000
Arab Fund for Economic and Social Development	1,440
Venezuelan Investment Fund[a]	1,448
Islamic Development Bank	2,640
Kuwait Fund for Arab Economic Development	3,663
OPEC Fund for International Development	4,000[b]
Saudi Development Fund	4,525

[a]Resources available for international financial cooperation are limited under bylaw to 15 percent of the fund's assets at the time disbursement is foreseen. The figure given is calculated as 15 percent of total resources of $9,654 million; actual commitments have, however, exceeded this figure.

[b]This figure represents total approved contributions, some of which is channeled through other international financial institutions.

TABLE 7.3

Paid-in Capital and Reserves of OPEC Aid Institutions
(in millions of dollars)

Institution*	Paid-in Capital and Reserves
Islamic Solidarity Fund	113
Arab Authority for Agricultural Investment and Development	232
Arab Monetary Fund	518
Abu Dhabi Fund for Arab Economic Development	565
Iraqi Fund for External Development	677
Arab Bank for Economic Development in Africa	799
OPEC Fund for International Development	1,008
Islamic Development Bank	1,065
Arab Fund for Economic and Social Development	1,074
Venezuelan Investment Fund	1,448
Kuwait Fund for Arab Economic Development	3,381
Saudi Development Fund	4,033

*Not reported: Libyan Bank, Iran Organization.

STRUCTURE, OBJECTIVES, DEVELOPMENT
PHILOSOPHY, AND LENDING POLICIES OF
MIDDLE EAST DEVELOPMENT FUNDS

National Development Funds

The most salient characteristic of all the national funds is that
they are first and foremost foreign policy instruments of their respective countries, and as such they are political in nature. This nature
is also reflected in their organization, particularly in the composition of top management. The degree of political control over their
operations, however, differs from country to country. There also
seems to be a correlation between the age of the organization, its
level of expertise, and its degree of political control. For instance,
the KFAED exhibits less political control than the ADFAED does. At
the same time, degree of political control also reflects the general
nature of government and society in each of the four countries having
national development funds.

Among the national funds, Kuwait's seems to have become fairly
autonomous as well as influential, particularly on decisions relating
to economic and financial issues. But even in this case, the composition of top management ensures that KFAED policies and operations
conform to and advance Kuwait's national interests. For instance,
until 1974 the chairman of the KFAED board of directors was the
minister of oil and finance. A law passed in 1974 made the prime
minister the chairman of the board, but allowed him to delegate part
of his powers to the minister of oil and finance, and in practice he
has done so.

The organizational structures of the national funds closely resemble one another, primarily because most of them were modeled
after Kuwait's fund. The KFAED organization consists of a board of
directors, an executive director, and a professional staff in charge
of different departments falling into three major categories: project
evaluation and lending, research, and financial and other administrative functions such as public relations and legal services. Some of
the national funds also have investment units in charge of managing
their portfolios, but such departments do not make major decisions.

Despite constant progress, one major structural problem of
these funds is lack of a sufficient number of trained, indigenous per-
sonnel. Thus, all of them must rely to a great extent on outside consultants and experts, particularly for project evaluation. This lack
of expertise has a considerable and often negative impact on lending
policies. For example, the funds essentially have been the receivers
of established ideas and conventional wisdom in the development field,

rather than the creators and initiators of new ideas and approaches potentially more suitable to regional conditions.

The primary objective of the national funds as foreign policy instruments of their respective countries is to advance national interests both within the region and beyond it. Advancing the economic and social development of regional and other developing countries is thus a secondary (albeit important) objective. The national interests served by these funds closely resemble those that development assistance programs set up by the industrial nations have traditionally been expected to promote, from the generation of political goodwill to the encouragement of a favorable investment climate among the recipients of aid. Some of the Gulf of Suez funds also see their efforts as contributing to the safeguarding of national security, in part by neutralizing potential rivals and adversaries.

In addition to these basic objectives, there are other aims that national funds pursue or at least claim to pursue. These aims include advancement of Arab economic development and increased inter-Arab economic cooperation, with the ultimate purpose of accelerating the process of Arab economic integration; and achievement of the aspirations of Third World countries and establishment of a so-called New International Economic Order (NIEO). In practice, however, these considerations have little impact on day-to-day operations, although they do provide an ideological framework and help to legitimize the way the funds operate.

The operations of the national funds demonstrate a lack of real commitment to, or strong preference for, any particular development philosophy, although declarations and policy statements made by their top management—and in some cases by their charters as well—do strongly reflect the dominant currents of Third World opinion about development issues. These positions are also replete with Arab nationalist themes, such as the need for economic integration of Arab countries.

Yet the record of the funds' operations does not show a consistent pattern of lending aimed at gradual but systematic achievement of declared goals. This discrepancy is not due to a conscious policy of deception. Rather, in addition to certain political conditions (such as differences among Arab countries), it is caused by a number of factors, particularly the following:

1. Lack of a sufficient indigenous base of technical expertise. Because these funds lack the technical capacity to assess independently the merits of approaches and to decide what projects could indeed advance their objectives, they tend to accept the views of existing international development institutions, or of consultants who come from essentially the same philosophical mold.

TABLE 7.4

Fund Disbursement by Sector of Recipient Economy

| Fund | Percentage of Disbursement Received by Sector | | | | | Total Disbursement (millions of dollars) |
	Agriculture	Industry	Energy	Public Utilities	Infrastructure*	
Kuwait Fund for Arab Economic Development	18.3	24.4	26.3	—	31.0	2,526
Abu Dhabi Fund for Arab Economic Development	10.6	51.7	—	23.6	11.1	901
Arab Fund for Economic and Social Development	10.6	15.6	23.7	14.4	35.7	1,235
Saudi Development Fund	21.3	3.3	20.4	12.3	42.6	4,159

*Includes communications, transport, and mining.

TABLE 7.5

Abu Dhabi Fund for Arab Economic Development Loan Commitments, 1978-79

Country	Amount of Loan (in millions of United Arab Emirates dirhams)	Percentage of Total Project Cost	Project
Bangladesh	60.0	23.3	Power system
Comoro Islands	4.0	100.0	Reconstruction of Anjuan Airport
Lesotho	3.0	100.0	Technical studies for Lesotho Airport
Malagasy	16.0	—	Power project
Maldives	8.0	11.0	Expanding Heluli Airport
Malta	28.0	13.0	Port development
Mauritania	40.0	8.0	Kifa–Naama Highway
	80.0	6.0	Gulub iron mining
Morocco	40.0	12.0	Gharb agricultural project
North Yemen	40.0	16.0	Taaz water and sewage system
	5.0	46.3	Financing Wadi Siham studies
Oman	663.0	42.0	Developing southern oil fields
Senegal	4.0	100.0	Technical studies for two dams
Seychelles	0.8	100.0	Ice plant
	3.3	32.0	Power plant
Sudan	84.0	37.0	Cotton spinning
Tunisia	218.8	40.0	Fertilizer project
Uganda	2.5	44.0	Renovation of textile plant

TABLE 7.6

Kuwait Fund for Arab Economic Development Loans, 1979–80

Country	Amount of Loan (in millions of Kuwait dinars)	Interest (in percent)	Maturity Years	Grace Years	Project
Arab					
Mauritania	12.90	3.0	24.0	6.3	Guelbs iron ore
Bahrain	6.16	4.0	16.7	2.7	North Sitra industrial area
South Yemen	4.00	1.5	19.9	3.9	Riyan Airport
Oman	2.00	4.0	17.7	3.7	Khuwair town infrastructure
North Yemen	2.00	2.5	36.5	6.5	Wadi Rima II
Djibouti	1.50	1.5	20.0	5.0	Dairy plant
Sudan	1.30	3.0	27.8	2.8	Rahad roads
Subtotal	29.86				
Asian					
Thailand	6.00	4.0	24.0	4.0	Bang Pakong power
Malaysia	5.50	5.5	19.2	5.2	Trengganu hydroelectric
Indonesia	5.00	4.0	19.3	4.3	Belawan–Morawa highway
Turkey	3.00	4.5	19.0	3.0	Istanbul water pipeline
Vietnam	2.90	3.0	24.5	4.5	Dau Tieng irrigation
Maldives	1.50	3.5	9.5	2.5	Merchant shipping
Sri Lanka	0.57	4.0	14.8	1.8	Urea fertilizer
Subtotal	24.47				
African					
Tanzania	5.00	4.0	22.8	4.8	Mufindi pulp and paper
Mali	4.20	2.0	24.3	4.3	Hambori–Gao road
Niger	3.00	4.0	20.2	4.2	Anou-Araren electric power complex, phase I
Mauritius	1.50	4.0	18.0	4.0	Champagne hydroelectric
Gambia	1.40	2.0	19.5	2.5	Development of river wharves
Subtotal	15.10				
Other					
Cyprus	2.50	5.0	17.4	5.4	Vasilikos–Pendaskinos irrigation
Total	71.93				

2. Fear of being accused of interfering in the domestic economic policies of recipient countries. The funds are genuinely concerned that if they strongly advocate a particular development philosophy, they will be accused of interfering in the process of economic planning and development.

3. Financial prudence. A basic conservatism argues against embracing untested approaches.

But even though the national funds do not seem to be committed to any particular development philosophy, a combination of factors has created a pronounced bias in favor of traditional development philosophies. Thus, for example, not only have they generally tended to emulate the World Bank and its lending priorities, but also to a great extent they have followed the shifts taking place in these priorities. For example, the funds' willingness to finance certain agricultural programs reflects the World Bank's attitudes.

All the national funds also demonstrate a strong bias in favor of project financing, although some of them—notably KFAED—have recently begun considering program lending. Among projects there is a strong bias in favor of infrastructure, and the funds are reluctant to finance social projects such as health, education, or population control (although they have financed a few) primarily because of the financial risks involved. Most of the funds also favor cofinancing, particularly in non–Arab, developing countries. In addition, they give priority to projects that have already been evaluated by reputable international or regional development institutions. The funds generally limit their financing to the foreign exchange costs of products and, except on rare occasions, they do not provide financing for local costs. Moreover, in general they only finance a certain percentage of the total cost, which in some cases could be as low as 10 percent.

Conditions of the loans and how much they concede vary according to the type of project (agricultural and social projects get more favorable terms) and the economic and financial situation of the recipients. Normally, the loans bear an interest rate between 1.0 and 1.5 percent and 7.0 percent, have a grace period of between three and five years (longer in exceptional cases), and have a maturity of up to twenty-five years (this can also be longer). See Tables 7.4-7.6 for sectoral breakdowns of loans and examples of projects financed.

Regional Development Funds

The only true regional fund in the Middle East is the Arab Fund for Economic and Social Development (AFESD). However, in view of their strong Middle East connections, the Islamic Development Bank (IsDB), the Arab Bank for Economic Development in Africa (BADEA), and the OPEC Fund for International Development will also be discussed briefly.

The Arab Fund for Economic and Social Development

The organizational structure of AFESD closely resembles that of the national development funds, except that it also has a board of governors to reflect its multinational character. Consisting of one governor and one alternate governor appointed by member states, the board is the fund's highest policy-making organ. Its professional staff is composed of nationals of member countries, and in its staffing policy the fund applies the principle of proportional representation.

Like the national development funds, AFESD faces a shortage of indigenous experts, and thus has had to rely to a great extent on outside experts. Yet, it has been trying to attract Arab experts, including expatriate Arabs, to enlarge its pool of technical expertise.

As an important symbol of Arab unity, the stated objective of the AFESD is to encourage Arab economic cooperation in ways that would facilitate greater Arab economic integration and, ultimately, Arab economic unity. Deriving from this underlying purpose are the following objectives: development of the infrastructure of Arab economies; promotion of investment opportunities for surplus Arab capital in the Arab region, particularly in productive sectors; and attraction of expatriate Arab professionals to the Arab region.

The AFESD development philosophy and lending policies derive from these principal objectives and the requirements for achieving them. For instance, the commitment to promoting inter-Arab cooperation creates a bias in favor of projects that involve two or more countries. The importance of the development of infrastructure in Arab countries in turn argues for giving priority to such projects. To the AFESD, the definition of infrastructure is broad enough to include human as well as physical dimensions. Therefore, a principal objective of the fund is to contribute to development of the human infrastructure of the Arab region.

In view of this objective, one major fund study seeks to identify areas of critical manpower shortages in the major production sectors and to determine possible remedies, among which may be the establishment of training centers to meet the member countries' requirements for technical and professional cadres. Meanwhile, the fund has granted numerous scholarships and has financed the advisory services of consultants for its members. See Tables 7.7 and 7.8 for specific data on these activities.

TABLE 7.7

Arab Fund for Social and Economic Development Activities, 1972–79

	1972	1973	1974	1975	1976	1977	1978	1979	Situation as of December 31, 1979
Loans									
Number of loans	–	–	8	11	14	15	–	6	54
Total amount (millions of Kuwait dinars)	–	–	33.700	56.100	98.200	103.900	–	26.200	318.100
Average amount per loan (millions of Kuwait dinars)	–	–	4.200	5.100	7.000	6.900	–	4.400	5.900
Total disbursements (millions of Kuwait dinars)	–	–	1.809	11.753	18.285	24.681	61.822	36.967	155.317
Technical assistance (millions of Kuwait dinars)									
Total amount	–	–	0.125	0.115	0.628	0.805	0.366	0.200[a]	2.239[b]
Total disbursements	–	–	0.125	0.112	0.159	0.623	0.278	0.169	1.466
UN–AFESD Joint Program (millions of Kuwait dinars)									
Fund allocations	–	–	–	–	1.700	–	–	–	1.700
Amounts disbursed	–	–	–	–	0.115	0.093	0.122	0.051[d]	0.381
UN allocations	–	–	–	–	2.200	–	–	–	2.200
Amounts disbursed	–	–	–	–	0.099	0.179	0.189	0.094	0.561
Authorized capital	100.000	–	102.500	400.000	–	–	–	–	400.000
Subscribed capital	81.010	–	18.850	2.190	87.460	180.930	–	14.700	385.140

(continued)

85

TABLE 7.7 (continued)

	1972	1973	1974	1975	1976	1977	1978	1979	Situation as of December 31, 1979
Paid-up capital	15.440	6.291	14.219	16.079	47.618	32.227	33.001	37.775	202.650
Total income	0.593	0.984	2.924	3.706	5.929	10.277	11.331	14.696	50.440
Total expenditures	0.045	0.562	0.831	0.928	1.449	2.107	2.199	1.997	10.118
Income surplus (millions of Kuwait dinars)	0.548	0.422	2.093	2.778	4.480	8.170	9.132	12.700	40.322
General reserve	0.055	0.042	0.197	0.266	0.448	0.817	0.913	1.270	4.008
Additional reserve	0.493	0.380	1.536	2.397	3.011	4.211	6.526	10.602	29.156
Foreign currencies and investments reserve	—	—	0.235	—	0.278	2.244	1.204	0.625	4.586
Technical aid	—	—	0.125	0.115	0.743	0.898	0.488	0.203	2.572
Number of member countries	17	17	17	20	21	21	21	21	21
Number of recipient countries	—	—	7	8	10	11	—	6	14
Professional staff	—	16	24	28	39	53	45	30	30

[a]Figures include KD145,000 approved during 1979 but not yet allocated.
[b]Includes KD258,000 savings of which KD28,000 were reallocated to the Arab Institute for Statistics.
[c]The fund provides in-kind technical assistance worth KD1 million.
[d]Includes KD48,000 administrative expenses of the UN-AFESD Joint Program.

Source: Reprinted with permission from Arab Fund for Economic and Social Development, Annual Report, 1979.

TABLE 7.8

Trends in Lending by Sector, 1974-79
(in millions of Kuwait dinars)

Sector	Loans	Percentage of Total
Infrastructure		
Transport and telecommunications	114.1	35
Electric power and energy	78.1	25
Water supply and sewerage	46.4	15
Subtotal	238.6	75
Economic		
Industry and mining	53.5	17
Agriculture and settlement	26.0	8
Subtotal	79.5	25
Total	318.1	100

Source: Reprinted with permission from Arab Fund for Economic and Social Development, Annual Report, 1979.

The Islamic Development Bank

This bank had its origins in a declaration of intent by the Conference of Finance Ministers of Islamic Countries held in Jiddya, Saudi Arabia, in December 1973, and it became fully operational in October 1975. It has 32 member states and an organization similar to other such institutions. It, too, suffers from a shortage of trained professional staff, and at its beginning had to borrow staff from the Asian, African, and World banks.

The underlying purpose of the IsDB is to foster the economic and social progress of its members and other Muslim communities, in accordance with the principles of the Sharia (Islamic law), by intensifying cooperation among Muslim countries. It is also supposed to encourage research in Islamic economics to enable Muslim countries to adjust their economic structure and planning to the requirements of Islamic law.

As far as the bank's development philosophy and lending policies are concerned, except for the impact of Islamic principles, it does not adhere to any rigid guidelines. In fact, perhaps more than any

TABLE 7.9

Total Financing Approved by the Islamic Development Bank, 1976–79

(in millions of Iraqi dinars)

Type of Financing	1396 H. (1975–76)	1397 H. (1976–77)	1398 H. (1977–78)	1399 H. (1978–79)	Total
Project	13.45	99.74	81.41	119.25	313.85
Trade	–	43.61	139.64	262.43	445.68
Total	13.45	143.35	221.05	381.68	759.53

TABLE 7.10

Amount Approved by the Islamic Development Bank for Project Financing, Classified according to Type of Financing, 1976–79

(in millions of Iraqi dinars)

Type of Financing	Number of Projects	1399 H. (1978–79)	Number of Projects	Total since Inception
Loans	6	33.74	24	127.11
Equity	9	44.78	24	124.82
Leasing	5	39.05	7	54.27
Profit sharing	–	–	1	4.27
Technical assistance	6	1.68	13	3.38
Total	26	119.25	69	313.85

Source: Islamic Development Bank, Annual Report, 1979.

TABLE 7.11

Sectoral Distribution of Financing by the Islamic Development Bank, 1976–79

Sector	Total through 1979 (in Iraqi dinars)	Proportion of Total (in percent)
Industry and mining	45.1	52.1
Transport and communications	27.7	25.2
Utilities	11.2	8.0
Agriculture	10.4	7.9
Social services	2.3	4.2
Other	2.3	2.6

TABLE 7.12

Amount Approved for Project Financing by the Islamic Development Bank, Classified according to Sector, 1978–79
(in millions of Iraqi dinars)

Sector	1399 H. (1978–79) Amount Approved	Percentage of Total Approved	Total through End 1399 H. (1978–79) Amount Approved	Percentage of Total Approved
Agriculture	9.45	7.9	32.48	10.4
Industry and mining	62.20	52.1	141.58	45.1
Transport and communication	30.02	25.2	86.87	27.7
Utilities	9.49	8.0	35.17	11.2
Social services	5.04	4.2	10.43	3.3
Other	3.05	2.6	7.32	2.3
Total	119.25	100.0	313.85	100.0

of the institutions discussed above, the IsDB approach is flexible and multifaceted.

The influence of Islamic law, however, means that the bank prefers equity participation in productive projects or profit-sharing arrangements. Moreover, the bank's loans are free of interest and carry only an administrative charge determined according to individual cases.

Nevertheless, the bank's approach has also been affected by dominant development philosophies. Thus, its declared policy is to participate in projects that "would contribute to the development of economic and social infrastructure of its member countries." However, because the term social infrastructure is vague, the end result is an emphasis on traditional infrastructure projects. The IsDB has also participated heavily in industrial projects, including mining. And it extends some program loans.

The IsDB is involved as well in a number of other financial support operations, such as foreign trade financing. Most of this activity so far has involved the financing of imports of crude oil and other petroleum products. The declared objective of this operation is to promote trade among member countries, particularly in capital goods, but in practice it has mainly been used to ease its members' oil burden.

The IsDB extends technical assistance, mostly in the form of service financing of consultants and other experts for feasibility and preinvestment studies. Moreover, it can establish and operate special funds, including trust funds (for example, the Islamic Solidarity Fund). It is authorized to accept deposits and to raise funds in any other manner, as well as to invest funds not needed in its operation.

In fact, the IsDB is an Islamic financial institution that is also involved in development financing; it is not a development fund in the narrow sense of the term. Thus, projected bank operations for the period 1980-81 show a dramatic shift toward foreign trade financing, mostly in crude oil and petroleum products. See Tables 7.9-7.12 for specific figures on IsDB financing activities.

The Arab Bank for Economic
Development in Africa

The decision to establish BADEA was reached at the Sixth Arab Summit Conference, held in Algiers in November 1973, and the bank began operating in 1975. All its members are Arab countries, although all its beneficiaries are African countries. Indeed, the BADEA is a significant symbol of the intensive interaction between Middle East and other developing countries, as Table 7.13 illustrates. The organizational structure of the BADEA resembles that of the other institutions discussed earlier in this chapter.

TABLE 7.13

Arab Bank for Economic Development in Africa Beneficiaries,
1975–80

1975

Benin
Cameroon
Congo
Ghana
Madagascar
Niger
Senegal
Tanzania
Togo/Ghana/Ivory Coast
Zaire

1976

Burundi
Gambia
Kenya
Mali
Mauritius
Rwanda
Sierra Leone
Upper Volta
Zambia
PANAFTEL[c]

1977

Cameroon
Ghana
Guinea
Liberia
Madagascar
Mali
Rwanda
Senegal
Tanzania

1978

Benin
Botswana
Burundi
Chad
Guinea Bissau
Lesotho
Liberia
Niger
Uganda[a]
Zaire
BDEAC[b]
PANAFTEL[c]

1979

Angola
Cape Verde
Comoros
Gambia
Guinea
Kenya
Lesotho
Mali

1980

Botswana
Burundi
Cameroon
Comoros
Mozambique
Senegal
Seychelles
Sierra Leone
Tanzania

---

[a]One loan and one grant.
[b]Banque Development Etats Afrique Centrale.
[c]Pan-African Telecommunications Network.

The bank's underlying objective is political: to win African friendship for the Arabs by contributing to African development, principally through concessional financing, encouragement of Arab and international investment in Africa, technical assistance, and co-ordination of Arab-African cooperation in economic development.

As far as development philosophy is concerned, the BADEA claims to be nonnormative and flexible, especially because of the complexity of the development planning process, the failure of past strategies, and the magnitude of African needs. Yet, the bank's operations initially emphasized infrastructure, although agriculture now receives equal emphasis. In 1975 the BADEA lent $52 million for infrastructure projects, and $11.6 million for agriculture; in 1978 infrastructure accounted for $24.1 million, and agriculture accounted for $27 million. The bank has also shown some flexibility in meeting emergencies. Within this general framework, the BADEA tries to keep in mind priorities set by the United Nations or other international organizations, as well as those of African countries themselves.

Most BADEA lending operations are for projects. The bank prefers cofinancing arrangements, particularly with other Arab or OPEC institutions, as well as with the African Development Bank, the European Development Bank, and the World Bank. It also tries to maintain a balance between East African and West African countries, while nevertheless favoring countries with lowest per capita incomes.

The concessionality of BADEA loans is quite high, with no rate of interest thus far exceeding 7 percent, and that rate has applied only to projects of rapid gestation when loan repayments are financed out of the proceeds of production made possible by the bank's funding. Loans have a grace period of up to 5 years and a maturity of between 15 and 25 years. In order to promote investment in Africa, the BADEA issues guarantees for the benefit of African and Arab institutions. It also tries to help Arab and African enterprises through its procurement policy, provided that service, quality, and performance do not result in a cost penalty of more than 10 percent. See Table 7.14 for a breakdown of BADEA loans by sector.

The bank has also administered resources of the Special Arab Aid Fund for Africa (SAAFA), which was established in 1974 to help African countries with their oil-import problems. In 1977 SAAFA resources were transferred to the BADEA and became part of its capital. By 1978 all the commitments made from SAAFA capital were disbursed—a total of $360 million.

TABLE 7.14

Arab Bank for Economic Development in Africa Loans by Sector, 1975–80
(cumulative amounts in millions of U.S. dollars)

Year	Agriculture		Industry		Infrastructure		Energy	
	Number of Projects	Amount Loaned	Number of Projects	Amount Loaned	Number of Projects	Amount Loaned	Number of Projects	Amount Loaned
1975	3	11.60	2	18.00	5	42.00	—	—
1976	7	29.40	2	18.00	9	71.10	2	15.00
1977	9	41.60	5	42.84	11	84.30	4	31.00
1978	14	56.25	7	52.54	15	101.90	6	41.92
1979	15	58.65	8	57.54	21	138.57	6	41.92
1980	17	77.15	10	77.54	25	170.82	7	43.12

The OPEC Fund for International Development

The collective OPEC aid organization was first established in 1976 under the name OPEC Special Fund (OSF). As initially envisaged, the fund was an international special account, owned collectively by the contributing parties (all of which belonged to OPEC), and hence was different from other special accounts because it was not owned by the institution whose name it carried.

In 1980 the OSF was elevated into an international agency for financial cooperation and assistance with an international personality of its own, a change whose impact is not yet clear. In the words of the fund's assistant secretary-general, the OPEC Fund for International Development (as it was renamed) "might undergo cosmetic or even substantial change." The fund's initial capital was $800 million, which was replenished twice, bringing its total capital to $4 billion.

When the OPEC Fund for International Development was first established, it was thought to be a short-lived facility and therefore was not given an elaborate administrative structure. It still has a small staff; but if it is to become a full-fledged development institution (by adding a loan-floating function, for example), then it would have to upgrade its professional and technical capability.

The establishment of the OPEC Fund for International Development was the culmination of efforts by OPEC countries to demonstrate their collective solidarity with other developing countries. Initially, some OPEC countries wanted to establish an organization with much larger resources, but inter-OPEC political and other differences made this impossible.

By 1975, however, pressure on OPEC countries to clarify their stand on international economic issues became very strong, as did pressure on OPEC relations with developing countries. Thus, the meeting of OPEC heads of state in Algiers endorsed developing-country efforts to shape a New International Economic Order (NIEO). As a result, the fund's overriding objective is to contribute to closing the global development gap and to creating the NIEO.

At least superficially, the fund has a more clearly defined development philosophy than many other such institutions, favoring a basic-needs approach. Moreover, in selecting projects it is supposed to give priority to those that alleviate income disparities and regional differences, reduce the dependence of recipient countries on imported energy, involve other OPEC aid agencies as cofinanciers, and increase the volume of trade and the mobility of production factors among developing countries.

The fund's lending policies have generally been flexible, and its operations involve balance-of-payments support, project loans, and program loans. Balance-of-payment support loans are interest free,

TABLE 7.15

OPEC Fund Balance-of-Payments Support Loans, 1980
(in millions of U.S. dollars)

Country	Amount
Africa	
Mali	6.00
Upper Volta	6.00
Mauritania	5.50
Tanzania	5.00
Madagascar	5.00
Senegal	4.50
Benin	4.50
Niger	4.00
Mozambique	3.50
Rwanda	3.00
Guinea-Bissau	2.00
Mauritius	2.00
Cape Verde	1.50
Djibouti	1.50
Gambia	1.50
Lesotho	1.50
Botswana	1.00
Comoros	1.00
Sierra Leone	1.00
Seychelles	0.50
Subtotal	60.50
Latin America	
Nicaragua	10.00
Jamaica	7.00
Guyana	5.00
Barbados	1.50
Grenada	1.00
Dominica	0.50
Subtotal	25.00
Asia	
Maldives	1.00
Western Samoa	0.75
Subtotal	1.75
Total	87.25

TABLE 7.16

OPEC Fund Project–Lending Operations, Geographical and Sectoral Distribution of Loans Committed in 1980
(in millions of U.S. dollars)

Country	Energy	Agriculture and Agro–industry	Transpor–tation	Industry*	Public Utilities	Total Amount Loaned
Africa						
Congo	—	—	8.00	—	—	8.00
Sudan	—	—	7.70	—	—	7.70
Ghana	6.00	—	—	1.50	—	7.50
Tunisia	—	—	6.00	—	—	6.00
Somalia	—	5.50	—	—	—	5.50
Burundi	—	2.00	—	—	3.00	5.00
Liberia	5.00	—	—	—	—	5.00
Senegal	—	—	—	5.00	—	5.00
Tanzania	5.00	—	—	—	—	5.00
Angola	—	—	3.00	—	—	3.00
Subtotal	16.00	7.50	24.70	6.50	3.00	57.00

96

Asia

Bangladesh	31.00	—	—	—	31.00
India	20.00	—	—	—	20.00
Pakistan	10.20	—	—	—	10.20
Thailand	8.00	—	6.32	—	8.00
Burma	—	—	—	—	6.32
Sri Lanka	6.00	—	—	—	6.00
Yemen, PDR	—	—	—	4.00	4.00
Nepal	1.30	—	—	—	1.30
Subtotal	76.50	—	6.32	4.00	86.82
Latin America					
Honduras	5.00	—	—	—	5.00
Haiti	—	3.50	—	—	3.50
Subtotal	5.00	3.50	—	—	8.50
Total	97.50	10.00	31.02	7.00	153.02
Percentage of total	63.7	6.5	20.3	4.6	100.0

*Including development banks.

97

with only a 0.5 percent service charge, a grace period of 5 years, and a maturity of 25 years. The loans must be used for importing capital goods, spare parts, and other agricultural and industrial inputs for civilian production. To enhance the development impact of its balance-of-payments support program, the fund requires borrowers to set aside in local currency an amount equal to the fund's loan, to finance local development projects. See Table 7.15 for figures on the fund's balance-of-payments support loans in 1980.

The OPEC Fund for International Development began project lending in 1977. In selecting recipients, the fund takes into account four main variables: per capita income as an index of poverty, population as an indicator of size, deficit in current account as a measure of liquidity and financial problems, and net oil imports for 1973 as a sign of energy-import dependence. In selecting projects, the fund assesses the following factors: economic priorities of recipient countries, opportunities for cofinancing, and compatibility of projects with the fund's philosophy. Table 7.16 shows figures for project-lending operations in 1980.

The reason for this approach is obvious: the fund does not want to be accused of economic interference. Its preference for cofinancing is explained by limited resources, both human and financial. The fund has thus far seen its role as that of a "gap filler"—a position that could change, however.

In addition to lending operations, the fund acts as a coordinator for OPEC policies on a number of international economic issues, including the establishment of a common fund.

RECORD OF PERFORMANCE:
NATIONAL DEVELOPMENT FUNDS

Any assessment of the performance record of the national development funds should keep in mind the following factors:

That they belong to countries that either have recently become independent or that have newly become active in international affairs;

That they suffer from serious handicaps such as shortage of technical expertise;

That they are developing countries with no viable economic base other than oil, which is a nonrenewable asset, and thus despite their wealth they are concerned about their future economic prospects;

That they have come under sudden and heavy pressure from different quarters to disburse large sums of money in a relatively short period of time;

That they face the same problems in their development efforts as other regional and international institutions. These problems principally derive from unfavorable social, economic, and political conditions among the recipients.

Even allowing for these considerations, the performance record would have been better if the national funds had not assumed such large financial burdens. For example, extreme financial caution has led these funds to finance projects that generally have a good chance of finding funding elsewhere (such as infrastructure projects), whereas they have not financed projects that would have difficulty attracting capital from other sources (such as projects with a high social content).

Moreover, the funds may have been too concerned with national pride and prestige. For example, in view of the problems discussed earlier in this chapter, if the Persian Gulf countries had pooled their resources and had set up a joint fund, they would have been able to harness a larger share of local talent and thus create a nucleus of local technical expertise. This, in turn, could have fostered a more creative approach toward regional development problems. Even better, they could have allocated larger sums to the AFESD or to the OPEC Fund for International Development, which would have had the same beneficial impact. To be fair, however, this would require a high degree of political concord and a spirit of regionalism or internationalism that simply does not exist yet, not only in the Middle East but anywhere in the developing world.

Nevertheless, the national funds have learned from experience: there have been increased consultations and coordination of activities not only among the national funds, but also between them and other regional and international development institutions.

RECORD OF PERFORMANCE:
REGIONAL DEVELOPMENT FUNDS

The Arab Fund for Economic and Social Development has been hindered in achieving its objectives because of a number of problems, particularly those deriving from political differences and regional tensions; differences in patterns of development of the region's countries; and legacies of the past, such as different patterns of trade relations reflecting past colonial links. Thus, the AFESD has been unable to finance any regional project of real significance. Still, it has done considerable work in preparing the way for launching such projects should conditions permit. For example, in cooperation with the

United Nations Development Program (UNDP), the fund has financed and helped develop an integrated program for identifying and evaluating inter-Arab projects in a systematic way, and for undertaking related preinvestment and feasibility studies. It has also financed and contributed to the preparation of several other studies dealing with different aspects of Arab regional development.

A detailed analysis of AFESD activities leaves the strong impression that political and other problems, such as inter-Arab political disagreements, have forced the diversion of its resources from its central objectives to peripheral activities.

As far as the other development funds are concerned, their performance falls short of their ambitions also. For example, efforts by the BADEA have not generated a rush of Arab capital to Africa, nor has trade among Islamic countries increased dramatically as a result of IsDB efforts. In addition, the OPEC Fund for International Development has been unable to translate its philosophy into concrete projects.

This rather disappointing record of performance is partly the result of factors discussed earlier in this chapter and partly the result of insufficient financial resources compared with the magnitude of development needs of the Middle East and the Third World in general. But perhaps more important, the performance record is poor because these funds were principally a political response to a political challenge (namely, pressure from the international community) rather than the product of a coordinated, well-thought-out development strategy.

Nevertheless, in fairness to the Middle East countries, it should be stressed that the beneficiaries would have been worse off without the funds' efforts. Also, the experience of 30 years of development assistance in general has been disappointing, as demonstrated by the widening gap between developing countries and the rest of the world. Even the assumption that development assistance can solve Third World economic problems has, for some time now, been seriously questioned.

To sum up, the failure of Middle East development institutions is a shared responsibility, particularly in view of the fact that previously existing international institutions played a major role in helping them start up and instilled in them their own development philosophies.

CONCLUSIONS AND RECOMMENDATIONS

The most significant conclusion to be drawn from this discussion of Middle East development institutions is that, ideally speaking, consolidation of existing institutions and reform of their mode of operations would best serve the interests of the region. But because of a variety of factors—such as political differences and national ambitions—this is not possible in the foreseeable future. Thus, there is room for at least one more such institution in the region. It need not be competitive with existing banks and funds if some elementary precautions are taken. This is because most of the existing organizations are national, and as such, are part of the governmental apparatus of their respective countries. A new institution, in contrast, could be regional in membership and international in sources of capital. The only point of friction could arise with the AFESD, which is also a multinational institution, but even in this case conflict need not be inevitable.

Logically, there could be no competition with the IsDB because of its Islamic character, or with the OPEC Fund for International Development because of its international aspect, or with the BADEA because it is an African, not a Middle East, institution. However, in view of prevailing conditions in the Middle East (such as disagreement among the Arabs regarding relations with Israel), a new institution could initially generate skepticism and even a certain amount of hostility. For example, some countries could view it as an effort to weaken or dilute indigenous development efforts, or even worse, to prevent Arab economic integration.

Of course, it might be impossible to convince all the skeptics; moreover, some countries might remain hostile to the idea no matter what is done to allay their misgivings. But in time, particularly if the peace process is successful, the new institution could gain the acceptance and respect of a larger number of countries in the region. This could happen especially if it keeps in mind certain considerations, including the following:

It should be designed to symbolize a new kind of partnership between developing and industrialized countries, a partnership more along the lines of developing-country aspirations.

It should rely as much as possible on local talent, while at the same time serving as a center for the development of an indigenous pool of expertise, as well as for the dissemination of technical and managerial know-how in economic development.

It should be daring in its lending operations, and it should finance as much as possible projects that normally have difficulty in finding sources of financing.

It should finance projects that have a high social content or a rapid impact on popular welfare.

It should, as soon as (or wherever) conditions permit, contact the existing organizations and register its readiness and desire to cooperate and even to coordinate some aspects of its activities with them.

It should not justify its existence in terms of the failure of the existing institutions.

NOTES

1. "Le recyclage des excedents de l'OPEP," Conjuncture bulletin economique (Banque de Paris and des Pays-Bas), April 1980, p. 53.

2. Middle East Economic Digest 25, no. 6 (February 6, 1981): 2.

8

A DEVELOPMENT FUND FOR
THE NEAR EAST

ROBERT R. NATHAN
JEROME I. LEVINSON

Peace is not merely a cessation of hostilities. Just as a military victory or an armistice can prove to be temporary, continuing peace can also prove to be elusive. Nor is there an absolute polarity distinguishing peace from war. The conception of peace can vary greatly, being subject to tensions, conflicts of interest, ideologies, perceptions of security, intolerances, and value judgments among and between nations.

Vast expenditures for defense purposes are committed throughout the world year after year, and the levels increase or decrease as nations evaluate threats to their peaceful objectives. Proposed military budgets in the United States over the next few years are indicative of the fluctuations that can occur in the pursuit of security. It is now projected that in the United States, real defense expenditures (dollar outlays adjusted for inflation) will have increased by approximately 60 percent from 1980 to 1986, raising the ratio of the defense component of the federal budget from about 23 percent in 1980 to over 37 percent in 1986.

In the Near East, defense outlays are at untenable levels relative both to domestic resources to finance these programs and to expanding demands upon limited resources for more constructive purposes. For Israel and Egypt, as well as for other Near East countries, large defense disbursements have resulted in high indebtedness, both internally and externally, thus diverting these funds from urgent economic and social development purposes.

History has taught us that economic distress can be a significant force leading to hostilities among nations. High living standards
and economic progress may not guarantee peace, but economic and
social improvements can serve, even in marginal degrees, to reduce
the probabilities of war over time. Efforts to improve the economies
of nations like Egypt, Israel, Lebanon, Jordan, and Syria are no
doubt commendable, given the serious deficiencies in education, housing, and health, as well as large pockets of severe poverty and priva-
tion in that region.

It is important for the world and the Middle East as a whole to
accelerate, broaden, and effectively implement the process of peace.
There has already been too much bloodshed, not only in the wars between Israel and its Arab neighbors, but in hostilities between Arab
nations as well. Stability in the area is essential if further costly
wars are to be avoided and if the region is to enjoy the social, psychological, and economic benefits of peace.

The peace process encompassing Egypt and Israel would be
greatly reinforced and expanded if both countries could be confident
that the benefits will be substantial and widely shared within each nation. The perception that steps are being taken to improve standards
of living and that security will be enhanced by accelerated development could, in itself, create an increasingly favorable environment
for effective steps toward enduring peace.

There is an old saying that one cannot solve problems by throwing dollars at them. Certainly, dollars alone do not solve problems,
and in fact, they sometimes even aggravate them. But it is more true
that throwing rhetoric at problems without providing the necessary resources seldom, if ever, leads to real solutions.

In the aftermath of the Camp David Agreement, Egypt received
tangible economic benefits through the return of the Israeli-developed
Alma oil fields. These fields had been supplying 40 percent of Israel's domestic petroleum requirements. By 1980 they contributed over
30,000 barrels per day (b/d) of Egypt's 600,000 b/d total production.
Israel, in turn, received special help from the United States in undertaking the major costs of dismantling the military airfields constructed
by Israel in the Sinai and of reconstructing similar facilities on Israeli
territory.

Nevertheless, beyond these specific benefits, no form of special
economic assistance was available to parallel the political "track."
Instead, economic aid continued to be channeled through conventional
sources: the World Bank, the International Monetary Fund, bilateral
aid channels, and private capital markets.

On the contrary, those who rejected the peace between Israel and
Egypt—the Palestine Liberation Organization (PLO), Iraq, Jordan,

and Syria—were in fact rewarded with substantial monies by the Arab surplus-oil-producing countries, if only for the "protection" of those providing the resources. The economic incentive to join the peacemakers simply did not exist.

Obviously, the absence of war constitutes a powerful incentive to continue the peace process. But it remains a fact that one of the expectations from the peace treaty was that it would lead to an improvement in standards of living.

Given these considerations, it is now appropriate that a serious effort be made to establish an internationally supported instrument or mechanism whereby the benefits of peace in the Near East will be more firmly and fully ensured. This process should begin with a dramatic conception. A cautious approach will not suffice. However controversial or fiscally infeasible it might be for governments' budgets at this time, a dramatic approach could ultimately prove to be the best and most economical means for consolidating the peace. This chapter proposes the creation of a Near East peace and reconstruction fund. Such an institution could be created through an entity combining government commitments with private and public capital.

THE SCHEME

The scheme for creating a Near East peace and reconstruction fund consists of three elements. The first element involves the initial constitution, by the United States, at least one European nation, Israel, Egypt, and perhaps Lebanon, of a joint economic Near East peace commission whose members would be the ministers of finance of the respective countries. The second element involves the formation of a special-purpose investment bank, financed with private capital of interested investors without regard to nationality, for the purpose of identifying, developing, promoting, and financing projects that are economically feasible and that jointly contribute to the economic progress of the regional countries participating in the scheme. The third element involves the formation of a Near East peace, reconstruction, and development fund by interested governments (those participating as members of the joint economic commission). The fund's purposes will be to contribute to the financing of projects that are economically feasible and that contribute to regional priorities, and to provide insurance against political risk to private parties investing in these projects.

A Joint Economic Middle East
Peace Commission

The purpose of a joint commission would be to provide an official umbrella for the economic effort. The commission's members
would be ministers of finance, except in the case of the United States,
whose member would be the secretary of the treasury. As the private
investment corporation and the Near East development fund become
organized, the presidents of these institutions could also become
members of the commission. The commission would review at the
ministerial level the progress and problems of economically advancing the peace process, would determine priority areas in which the
investment effort could yield maximum benefit, would mobilize efforts
of the individual governments in support of the scheme, would encourage private investment, and would break bottlenecks within the respective governments that impede the effort.

Thus, the joint commission would represent a political commitment by participating governments to ensure top-level attention to the
supporters of the fund. There is a precedent for creating such a commission. In the aftermath of the 1973 oil-price increases, the United
States and Saudi Arabia organized a joint economic commission. The
United States was represented by its secretary of the treasury, and
Saudi Arabia was represented by its minister of state for finance and
national economy.

At that time, Saudi Arabia wanted the United States to undertake
major construction projects on a turn-key basis. The United States
wished to ensure the investment of substantial Saudi Arabian financial
surpluses in U.S. government securities. Through the joint commission, both of these objectives were accomplished: the Army Corps of
Engineers is supervising billions of dollars in construction projects
for Saudi Arabia, which has, in fact, invested billions of dollars in
U.S. government paper under terms especially designed for Saudi
Arabia. The joint commission, in effect, became the vehicle through
which the United States ensured continuous, official, top-level attention to economic and financial issues in which Saudi Arabia had an interest. It also ensured a systematic dialogue with Saudi Arabia on
financial and economic issues of mutual concern.

It is ironic that the United States effectively institutionalized a
process for resolving the economic and financial concerns of a country
that, in 1973, did it great economic harm, but that has shown little
interest in constituting a similar forum for the economic concerns of
countries involved in the peace process. True, in the Saudi case no
congressionally appropriated funds were involved. Saudi Arabia did,
however, levy a tax on U.S. oil consumers through the oil-price in-

creases, just as if such a tax had been legislated by the U.S. Congress. If the United States was prepared to assist Saudi Arabia in productively investing the resources drawn from oil consumers, it should be willing to invest resources to advance the peace process.

For the first two years, the joint economic Middle East peace commission should meet at six-month intervals. Meetings could take place on a rotating basis in each of the participating countries with the minister of the host country acting as chairman. A permanent secretariat consisting of a nominee from each country would ensure appropriate implementation of the projects. The secretariat would thus provide essential movement during the otherwise dead period of time it would take to organize the scheme's financing arms. As the corporation and the fund become operational, the joint commission would perform more of a political policy-making and review function than operational tasks.

What makes this scheme potentially unique is that it links to a common objective both a high-level political umbrella (the fund) and a private-financing vehicle.

Formation of a Special Investment Bank:
The Operating Entities

It is proposed that a separate entity be formed to directly channel private and public sources of capital. If a single entity were formed, the flexibility and initiative of the private investors could be potentially vitiated by the public-reporting and public-review requirements that inevitably accompany funds authorized by legislative bodies. Moreover, the operating styles of private-investment entities and publicly funded institutions are sufficiently different to warrant separate operations. At the same time, through the joint commission both entities would be assured highly visible political backing at the ministerial level and coordination of their objectives, policies, and operations.

A Near East Peace, Reconstruction,
and Development Fund

Why establish a new regional fund when the world is already awash with development institutions and most existing ones can hardly engender domestic political backing in the parliaments of the industrialized countries? This new institution would be the only such initiative directly and specifically tied to a clearly defined political objec-

tive: consolidating through specific economic linkages the peace
agreement between Egypt, Israel, and any other countries choosing
to join the process. Existing multilateral development institutions
cannot achieve the objectives envisioned through the creation of a
Near East peace, reconstruction, and development fund (NEPRDF).
The World Bank is universal in scope; hence, operations in Egypt must
meet overall World Bank policy and standards and cannot be tailored
to the particular political circumstances of the Egyptian-Israeli situation. Moreover, since Israel has been "graduated" from eligibility
status for World Bank lending, the type of projects that yield simul-
taneous benefits to both countries cannot be undertaken in a coordinated
fashion. Similarly, the Agency for International Development (AID)
bilateral program is, by definition, a program between Egypt and the
United States, and to a lesser extent, between Israel and the United
States. It cannot build cross-linkages between Egypt and Israel and
other Near East nations. In their present form and orientation, the
Islamic Development Bank, the Kuwait Fund for Arab Economic Development, and the Arab Bank for the Economic Development in Africa are incapable of contributing to the peace process.

In contrast, the NEPRDF could be staffed to a significant degree
by Israelis, Egyptians, and Lebanese and could engage in a continuous
process of project identification and preparation and financing arrangements, which would amount to a form of planning with regional impacts.
As the projects are implemented with mutual benefits to the peoples of
both countries, there would be created over the next ten years a habit
of joint planning and a nexus of concrete economic ties, which would
constitute a reinforcing element to the political peace agreement. Although less ambitious than the European Economic Community, the
political effect could be much the same: creation of institutions that
provide the means of continuous involvement in resolving common
economic problems, and forging of economic ties that give each country a greater tangible stake in maintaining and advancing the peace
agreement. These objectives are not on the agenda of other universal
institutions such as the World Bank or bilateral entities such as the
Agency for International Development. But they could and should be
on the agenda of a regional development entity evolving in the Near
East. The staffing of top-level positions would have to be negotiated.

Specifically, the fund could have the following characteristics.
Its resources would be used to finance projects and programs that are
economically feasible and that benefit two or more countries in the region, or that can be shown to have demonstrated to the region's peoples
that the peace process has measurably improved the quality of their
lives. The fund's resources would also be used to insure private foreign investors engaged in similar projects against political risk such

as expropriation, inconvertibility of currencies, war, and civil insurrection.

The fund's resources would consist of paid-in capital; agreements to subscribe further capital to the fund (callable capital); sums received as earnings; and funds made available by contributing countries, whether members of the fund or not, in other forms (for example, funds given in trust for general or specific purposes).

In order to be credible, the fund must be perceived to have significant resources available to it in the near future for a reasonable period of time. Therefore, it would need to have an initial, publicly binding commitment of not less than $15 billion over a five-year period, of which $1.5 billion (10 percent) should be paid in at the start.

Not all of this amount would need to be made available in equal installments. Given the start-up time of the fund, early installments could be of a lesser amount. Later installments could be estimated on an as-needed basis and evidenced in encashment schedules, which could be reviewed and changed on a periodic basis.

The participating nations could execute an agreement establishing the fund, which would possess an independent juridical personality. The fund would continue in effect for 25 years unless renewed or terminated by common consent of all participants at an earlier date. The form of a fund has been chosen to emphasize the enterprise's limited purposes: advancing the peace process through economic linkages and bringing near-term benefits to citizens of the participating countries. As was noted above, linkage to political objectives would differentiate the fund from the more conventional multilateral development banks, whose objectives are more indeterminate and generalized. The 25-year term is based upon an estimated average amortization life of the loans that would vary depending upon the projects being financed, and upon the probable time needed to ensure continuity of regional cooperation and coordination.

The fund's ultimate authority would be a board of directors consisting of representatives from each member country. Experience would determine frequency of meetings and criteria for full-time membership. The board would need to approve all loans, expropriation insurance policies, and operating-policy guidelines. Day-to-day management and operating decisions would remain the responsibility of the staff. Additional functions and operating procedures of the fund could entail the following:

The fund would be able to invest resources held for liquidity purposes and would have resort to capital markets with bond issues backed by the callable and paid-in capital of member countries.

The fund would be expected to provide technical assistance in the formulation of projects and to coordinate its financing role with existing multilateral and bilateral development efforts, as well as with the private-investment entity.

Preference would be given in the procurement of goods and services to suppliers in member countries of the fund. Goods and services to be financed would be acquired at the best price consistent with the requirements of quality and timeliness.

The fund would make investments on financial terms and conditions guaranteeing that it can cover all expenses, including financial costs, appropriately related to the risks it takes. These terms and conditions would also ensure the fund a surplus earnings that would enhance its credit for borrowing in the market and that would thus serve as a base for expanding its operations.

The fund would not provide subsidized services except when financed from its earned surpluses or from funds especially provided by donors for that purpose.

The fund would be audited annually by qualified accountants working in accordance with internationally accepted standards.

In contrast to conventional multilateral development institutions, the fund would not be expected to attempt to influence development policies, macro or sectorial, of the member countries in which projects are being financed except where such policies adversely impact the financial or economic feasibility of the project being financed or insured. While the fund would be governed by economic feasibility in determining projects to be financed or investments to be insured, due consideration should also be given to the degree and manner in which such projects advance acceptance of the peace process in the respective countries.

INSURING AGAINST POLITICAL RISK

Given the history of the area, insurance against political risk is necessary to attract foreign investors. A multilateral program such as the NEPRDF would help forge deeper ties in the Near East. If, for example, the proposal were based on a concept of pooled insurance, the United States and other nations could, through the fund, insure investment in Egypt, Israel, Lebanon, and other participating countries.

Insurance Operations

Insurance or guarantees would be available only to eligible investors, including any of the following: nationals of the fund's member countries, and nationals of potential member countries in the region. The investment must consist of new capital or technical skills (being contributed to a given project) that qualify as foreign under the laws of the host country.

Insurance would cover losses due to expropriation, inconvertibility, war, revolution, or insurrection. As a general rule, coverage would extend between seven and fifteen years. Expropriation would be defined to include "creeping" appropriation.

An insurance reserve of at least $100 million would be established at the outset, from which claims will initially be paid. Appropriate coverage would be established for each risk. In the case of convertibility, payments would be made at exchange rates in effect during the particular period of blockage claimed by the investor. Under expropriation, payments would generally be based on the value of the insured investment adjusted for earnings or losses. Payments may also be made for the loss of a portion of proved reserves in a project in which the investor has an interest.

In the event of a claim, the fund would require the investor to take all reasonable action that would help to mediate the loss. The fund's administrator would have full powers and the broadest flexibility to effect a recovery, including requiring the investor to conduct analyses and to undertake discussions.

The investors would be required to bear a portion of the insured risks in order to have a meaningful amount of their own resources at stake in the project.

A Private Investment Corporation

Some private investment entities have operated on a regional basis and have not fared well, specifically the Atlantic Community Development Group for Latin America (ADELA). Therefore, because of the need for a Near East private-investment entity to search out investment opportunities that benefit countries participating in the scheme, and to promote, organize, and finance economically viable projects beyond what is being done at present, the management of a new investment entity must be of high caliber in order to optimize the prospects for success. In the past, no group of investors had large enough stakes in the venture or were sufficiently motivated to take the lead in ensuring sound management of the enterprise. The perception that such ensurance would be built into the venture would probably be decisive—other things being equal—in attracting a broad base of foreign investors.

Among the principal functions of a new investment entity would be the financing of economically feasible projects. A private investment corporation could fulfill this function if it had the following characteristics:

The entity would concentrate on project and project-related financing of a kind not adequately addressed by existing institutions.

The entity would be empowered to engage in merchant-banking operations, equity investments, and credit extension.

The entity could commit its own resources for these purposes and would seek maximum participation by outside investors.

The entity would be responsible to its shareholders; it would operate under the laws and regulations of countries in which it is headquartered and conducts business; it would enjoy no special privileges; and its profits would be taxable, although tax incentives should be encouraged.

A firm decision on the size and nature of capital would be made after potential investors have been canvassed; but a bank—even a purely merchant bank—of less than $50 million capital would hardly be worth pursuing.

The entity would endeavor to earn an attractive return on capital and to avoid losses that impair earnings or capital.

The need to call up capital or increase shares would be determined by the board of directors.

The entity's investment and lending criteria would be guided by the need to achieve and maintain its own creditworthiness and to give confidence to its shareholders, as well as to contribute to economic growth in the region. The aim would be to have an asset portfolio giving the new entity a very high credit standing.

The entity would fund itself from worldwide financial markets. It could make loans and investments in any currency. Matters like country risk, hedging against foreign-exchange risk, liquidity, and capital adequacy would be decided by management, including the board of directors, based on private banking and investment principles within the framework of promoting sound development within the host countries.

The entity's capital must be sufficient to provide a solid base for its operations; the aim would be to build capital from profitable activities over the following years. Declaration, magnitude, and timing of dividends would be decided by the board of directors at management's recommendation. Investors could not expect dividends until profits were earned; loan contracts would be fulfilled promptly.

The entity could have headquarters in London or New York and offices in other countries if deemed appropriate. The venue of the entity would be decided by the shareholders.

The entity would aim to have a minimal staff of the highest professional quality and reputation, capable of evaluating project proposals from the viewpoint of private investors and of dealing effectively with private investors; full use would be made of existing private and public institutions in host and creditor countries.

The entity would aim to achieve the international financial standing needed to give its capital substantial leverage. In its early years, it would not be expected to achieve maximum levels of leverage because prime importance would be given to careful asset acquisition and minimization of loan losses. However, favorable experience should bring steady progress.

Loans made by the entity would probably average longer than the maturities of ordinary commercial banks; shorter maturities would be available for project- and trade-related purposes; general-purpose loans would be given lower priority. Portfolio diversification would be a guiding principle of lending and investing.

Immediate and ongoing commitments for a period of years will be required if the effort to establish a Near East private investment corporation is to be successful. Most important is the need to initiate actual steps and arrangements to translate the concept into realistic and ambitious actions within determined time schedules.

RESOURCES

One important consideration is to determine the size of financial commitments a NEPRDF will require. If the amount is not large enough to ensure significant results within a few years, much of the prospective benefits can be lost or dissipated, with frustration replacing hope and confidence. The amount should be related to the optimum level of external assistance that can be effectively absorbed for large projects common to countries in the region. To have the largest impact, commitments to the fund should cover projected needs for at least five years. At this stage it is difficult to suggest a precise figure, but at least $15 billion should be an appropriate initial goal. Pledges should not be contingent upon political developments. The resources must be additional to, not substitutes for, previously available assistance levels.

Consensus and support are needed now for an effective, internationally supported institution with adequate resources. The first task is to build understanding and sponsorship, especially in the United States and Western Europe. However, until the concept is adopted and encouraged by Near East states and by the more-developed nations, it will not become a significant reality. Although this effort may be expensive in a period of economic recession and budgetary constraint, we must ask ourselves whether it is a high price to pay compared with the alternatives, including the cost of further war in the Near East.

9

COMMENTARY: NEED AND RATIONALE FOR A NEAR EAST DEVELOPMENT FUND

FAWZI HABIB

In his statement of March 26, 1979, following the signing of the peace treaty, Prime Minister Begin said, "Peace . . . is sunshine. It is the advancement of man, the victory of a just cause, the triumph of truth. Let us not forget that in ancient times, our two nations (Egypt and Israel) met also in alliance. Now we make peace the cornerstone of cooperation and friendship." I stress the last sentence: peace as the cornerstone of cooperation and friendship.

Less than two years before, on November 20, 1977, President Sadat spoke to the Israeli Knesset, saying, "I come to you today on solid grounds to shape a new life and to establish peace. We all love this land—the land of God. We all, Moslems, Christians, and Jews, all worship God."

Indeed, peace is the cornerstone of cooperation and friendship; its establishment is conducive to betterment, to progress, and to a new life.

In Chapter 7 of this book, Shireen Hunter has given a complete account of development funds actually in operation in the Middle East. In Chapter 4, Fred Gottheil has reviewed Egypt's economic and political difficulties following the peace treaty with Israel: its isolation from other Arab states and the ensuing cutoff of all kinds of aid. I agree with Gottheil that the cost of five wars within a decade was massive, that Egypt's present problems are chronic and substantial but could be overcome through serious and concerted action. Clearly, technical and financial aid of all kinds and from any source is crucial to overcoming the economic and social ills of the poor countries of the region.

Several questions must be raised about a possible new development fund for the Middle East. Is there need for a regional development fund to serve countries and governments that are so widely divided? In terms of timing and existing differences, can a development fund be established to serve the interest of the region's "allied" nations as an initial core around which to build? And, finally, what could be expected of such a fund?

This chapter begins with a description of the region, making special reference to Egypt, Israel, and the Sudan. The views expressed are mine alone, and they do not necessarily represent the view of either the International Finance Corporation or the World Bank Group at large.

Conditions of deprivation that have divided the "have" countries and the "have-not" countries exist in much of the Near East, stretching from the Mediterranean Sea to the Indian Ocean and from Lebanon to equatorial Africa. In a region of 100 million people, the land is generally poor, lacks water, and has few minerals; the people lack technical skills and, until recently, capital. The people of the Middle East are poverty stricken, except for a tiny minority that enjoys sudden wealth. The countries range from Egypt—with a population in excess of 40 million—to the United Arab Emirates of the Persian Gulf— with only 350,000 people—and from highly industrial sophistication and modern technology in Israel to the isolated peoples of the Yemen who are just emerging from the Middle Ages. Their political systems vary from republics to monarchies, and their economies vary from state control to free enterprise. They share a largely common heritage and culture, and are predominantly Islamic; most share the Arabic language, although significant groups speak Persian, Turkish, Kurdish, and other languages. Much of the Middle East shares an assertion of Arab cultural identity, with common aims, beliefs, and ambitions, even though they do not agree on the best ways to fulfill them. All desire modernization and progress, with some fighting for wealth, while others resent the power the wealthy wield over them.

Despite the region's endowment with substantial oil riches, its average per capita gross national product (GNP) growth during the 1970s was less than 0.5 percent and is projected at zero level in the 1980s unless drastic internal and external development efforts are made. The region's average population growth rate was 2.6 percent during the 1970s and is projected to rise to 3.1 percent during the 1980s. The balance-of-payments deficit on current account for the region as a whole (excluding oil-producing countries) was huge, increasing from $4.6 billion in 1977 to $8.1 billion in 1979 and reaching over $10 billion in 1980.

For many Near East countries, the recent past has been a period of mounting external and internal difficulties. It now seems likely that many countries in the group face protracted economic and demographic pressure with little hope of widespread relief. Some of the major difficulties of the past few years have come from a generally unfavorable external environment reflecting deterioration in trade, particularly the increase in oil prices. On the domestic front, growth in real output was small. For the immediate future, a slight recovery in the rate of growth of real output and some stability in rates of inflation appear likely, at least in countries not engaged in actual warfare.

Substantial increases in external borrowing by some countries, associated with considerable reduction in the real value of their official reserves, has helped finance a slight increase in imports. Even the maintenance of the current mediocre rate of expansion in inflow of real resources from abroad is straining the international financial position of the non-oil-producing countries of the region. These strains cast a shadow over the countries' ability to accelerate growth of their imports during the next several years without further reduction in their meager reserve position in real terms, and especially in relation to imports. Indeed, the drain of war has taken its toll on the resources of some of the region's countries that have been heavily engaged in combat. In some, resources committed to basic-production needs were unfortunately diverted to finance military hardware.

The pattern and composition of bilateral and multinational aid to Near East countries have not been even. But at least for Egypt, the data in Table 9.1 suggest a significant worsening in its net position between 1976 and 1979.

Table 9.1 shows that after 1976 aid to Egypt from the Organization of Petroleum Exporting Countries (OPEC), previously in excess of $1 billion, ceased altogether. Concessional loans and grants were $1.3 billion less in 1979 than in 1977. In addition, Egypt's consolidated net-aid receipts, together with fiscal surplus, fell short of meeting its investment targets even if account is taken of foreign-exchange earnings resulting from growth in commodity exports, including oil, and from services and invisibles in the form of tourism, Suez Canal tolls, and remittances from nationals abroad—all of which were well-established sources reflecting, in part, domestic efforts.

The long-term challenge facing Egypt derives from the fact that comparable rapid growth can no longer be expected from these four sources. Although petroleum, Suez Canal revenues, workers' remittances, and foreign-capital inflows will continue to contribute valuable

TABLE 9.1

Aid to Egypt by Source, 1976-79
(in billions of dollars)

Source of Aid	1976	1977	1978	1979
Bilateral (from Organization of Petroleum Exporting Countries members)	1,022	882	508	32
Net from Development Assistance Committee countries	428	617	860	1,011
Net from all sources (concessional loans and grants)	1,798	2,613	2,267	1,294
Total recorded net flows of resources to Egypt (including banks and other market flows)	2,323	3,069	2,761	1,907

Source: Organization for Economic Cooperation and Development, 1980 Review, pp. 211-35.

resources to Egypt's development, rapid economic growth will likely depend increasingly on the performance of the domestic commodity-producing sectors, notably industry and agriculture. Such a change in the basic structure of Egypt's growth—from growth based on "natural resource" and "foreign resource" to growth based on domestic production of agricultural and industrial commodities—will require a fundamental shift in economic strategy and in the structure of domestic prices and incentives. Moreover, a massive growth in national savings will be required to finance the kind of investment program that could renew and expand Egypt's capital stock and lay the foundations for self-sustaining growth in the domestic economy.

Notwithstanding Egypt's grave problems, the present and future do hold opportunities. First, Egypt is the region's most industrialized country, commanding a well-trained labor force. But the defeat in 1967, the mounting defense burden thereafter, and the direct and indirect costs of the war in 1973 cost Egypt approximately $30 billion spent for the Arab cause.

The 1976 census estimated that 1.4 million Egyptians, nearly 4 percent of the population and 14 percent of the labor force, were largely employed in capital-surplus and Arab oil-producing countries. While the emigration of workers relieves domestic unemployment, continued economic growth will increase the demand for experienced and trained Egyptian labor now working abroad, workers whose skills and proficiency are strongly missed. This brain drain involves a costly loss of the investment made in education and training, all at a time when investment in human resources imposes a heavy burden on Egypt's financial resources. Furthermore, prolonged residence abroad of experienced workers and highly specialized professionals could result in a decline in their remittances over time.

Another consideration is the relationship between Egypt and the Sudan. In addition to a common cultural heritage, the Sudan and Egypt share a major resource, the Nile River. Centuries of ties bind the two countries; however, the role of Saudi Arabia has recently become crucial to any understanding of Egyptian-Sudanese relations. Saudi Arabia's objective, according to some sources, is to build Sudan's agricultural potential in order to supply the Gulf states with foodstuffs and to provide suitable terrain for profitable Saudi investments. Also, it is not in Saudi Arabia's interest to see the Sudan as a kind of agricultural hinterland to an industrializing Egypt.

Whether because of an interest in securing sources of agricultural products in the Sudan, or because of the military and political weight attached to Egypt, Saudi Arabia—as the richest of the Arab oil states—is likely to resume aid to Egypt and others once peaceful coexistence is established. Charity should start at home, and mass poverty could be a threat to the whole region's stability.

External assistance, albeit necessary at this stage of Egypt's development, is not a substitute for domestic efforts, nor should it be an endless process. It should be emphasized at this juncture that Egypt's fiscal and financial management showed a sharp and favorable trend in recent years, contributing significantly to the country's total investment.

As the donor countries' resource constraints intensify, owing to changes in foreign-aid policies or as a result of inflationary pressures, competition for funds will become more severe and the award of aid to the region's customary recipients will become difficult, partly because allotments may be based on individual merit or on geographical, sectoral, or other priorities.

A prerequisite to establishing a regional development institution is the desire and consent of two groups. On the one hand, countries in the region that would receive aid must be willing to organize, must make necessary analyses and applications, and must ultimately qualify to receive direct and nondirect financial aid. On the other hand, a second group made up of members within and outside the region must be willing to subscribe to such a common cause, to make their assessed contributions, to concede development loans on market terms, and to make grants and/or soft loans with the purpose of helping recipient countries to cope effectively with some of their problems under conditions of fiscal discipline and monetary stability.

But how can such an accord be reached between countries in a region so widely divided, with warfare between Iran and Iraq, with forces still occupying Lebanon, with the Arab-Israeli conflict unresolved, and with continuing tensions between Libya and Chad? Except for peaceful relations between Egypt and Israel on one side, and between Egypt and the Sudan on the other, all are divided.

Under existing circumstances, a new fund for the Near East would not be likely to attract broad membership from within the region. Given the urgency for development, however, it would be advisable to build the fund around a core of a few states, thus helping to cement existing peace efforts in the region. With the crying need for help and the need to organize it, legislative and legal delays should be kept at a minimum. It might also be more practical and timesaving to consider, for a start, the creation of a multinational consortium including members from outside the region to be concerned with program financing and national or multinational investments based on sectoral priorities. Just like a formal fund, a multinational consortium could aim at increasing the total flow of public and private capital to the "allied" members, not merely at diverting resources from existing channels. Such a policy would tempt some less enthusiastic potential members, fearful that new proposals of this kind might lead to duplication and waste, to join. Stimulating action may be further strengthened if investments are directed to a limited number of sectors, such as energy, agriculture, and basic industry.

This new consortium could be a major force in strengthening the mutually fruitful ties already formed between Egypt and Israel and could be useful in extending regional cooperation and assistance. Israel, with high technology and an organizing ability that has transformed deserts into blooming fields, could play a vital role in bringing technology to the face of the desert lands.

10

MIDDLE EAST WATER: VITAL RESOURCE, CONFLICT, AND COOPERATION

ADDEANE S. CAELLEIGH

The Middle East lacks no grounds for conflict. Differing religions, sects, and peoples vie for control of territory and national destiny in a region burdened with some of the globe's most hostile environments, and blessed with some of its most valuable resources. The nations of the area struggle with problems of government and development in an atmosphere of regional tension that periodically breaks into warfare, all the while under the scrutiny of Western nations anxious about oil supply and fearful of global confrontation spreading from local disputes.

In this context of decades-long hostility and centuries-old suspicions, Middle East peoples struggle with all the problems of young—and often poor—states. Rich or poor, Middle East countries face the difficulties of economic development that confront all nonindustrialized societies: issues of resource poverty, disruptive demographic growth, and rapid social change that would challenge the capacity of the most astute governments. Even with long-term economic planning, measured social change, and the benevolent cooperation of international institutions, these states would inherit social and economic crises. As it is, Middle East countries must find their way between the imperatives of technological development and their citizens' demands for culturally satisfying societies, with only the use of crude economic and social tools, flawed advice from friends, and their entrenched systems of administration and organization. In these respects, they resemble

their industrialized mentors, who must tackle different but equally
vexing economic and social woes. Unfortunately for Middle East countries, they must work out their development in a region of limited resources, with international boundaries often mandated by foreign powers and modern wars, and with political exigencies that sometimes
limit or forbid cooperation.

Clearly, the Middle East requires regional cooperation in order
to solve many of its development dilemmas, for many of its problems
recognize no ethnic, religious, or political boundaries. In considering possible starting points for regional cooperation, one basis immediately comes to mind. Water, not oil, is the Middle East's most
precious resource. Yet, discussions of Middle East conflict focus
on oil, and perhaps understandably so, for it is oil that has transformed not only the oil-rich Middle East states, but also the international political and economic systems linking the world's nations.

Nonetheless, the crucial resource in Middle East development
is, and always has been, water. Societies in the Middle East have
been limited to a scale of development measured by human ability to
control and distribute water. The twentieth century has seen remark-
able advances in the techniques of water retrieval and manipulation,
but very little change in the water resources available in the Middle
East. Ironically, the industrial development and social modernization these societies seek, which in some cases is made possible only
by oil exploitation, put the greatest strain on water supplies and pose
the gravest threat to future water sufficiency. Middle East countries
have some of the highest birthrates in the world, as well as disruptive
rural-to-urban migration, both of which require constantly increasing
water supplies. In addition, two goals of every Middle East society—
increases in agriculture and development of industrial capacity—place
substantial new demands on available water resources. The few costly
desalination projects now operating add little to total supplies, while
the retrieval systems capable of bringing up water from greater depths
and of pumping it greater distances hasten eventual water scarcity. [1]

Yet, few Middle East governments have consistent water planning, several bilateral water agreements have broken down, and no
regional plans exist—or are likely to exist soon—for cooperation in
the protection and distribution of the region's limited water.

Conflicts over water will inevitably complicate any attempts to
develop regional cooperative systems or agreements. For example,
the extent to which Israel is dependent on water resources in the occupied territories will be a major factor, implicit or explicit, in any
negotiations on the fate of the West Bank. Similarly, Turkey's and
Syria's damming of the Euphrates River allows diversion of water
that would otherwise reach major agricultural areas downstream in

Iraq. Considering the longstanding tensions between the rival Ba'athist governments of Syria and Iraq, the dams raise the possibility of Syria deliberately limiting water supplies to Iraq. In a different context, officials and analysts are increasingly concerned that Saudi Arabia is poisoning its scarce water reserves in its concerted effort to modernize and industrialize, just as they foresee that a successful bombing raid on Abu Dhabi's or Kuwait's desalination facilities would, for example, force immediate evacuation of a significant proportion, if not all, of the sheikhdom's entire population. Fighting in Lebanon between 1975 and 1982, for example, forced the abandonment of several small towns after their water systems were destroyed.

Each of these examples highlights in different ways the obstacles to development posed by the discrepancy between present water resources and future needs, the potential for international disputes over control of existing water supplies necessary to future development, and the vulnerability of these societies to disruption of water systems. Any understanding of the important role water resources are likely to play in future relations between Middle East states and in the development of regional economic cooperation must depend, first, on knowing where the critical points in water control and distribution lie, and second, on examining the potential for future conflict in disputes over these water supplies.

The details of water disputes are, of course, important to an understanding of the nature of a particular conflict between two states, but the focus in this chapter is on the sources of conflict over Middle East water resources rather than on the disputes themselves. Looking at two rivers that are vital to the prosperity of the states through which they flow—the Euphrates and the Jordan—provides a convenient way to highlight the nature of conflict over multinational river systems and the ways in which political antagonisms both prevent coordinated water development and, to a lesser extent, result from existing hostility over water rights.

THE EUPHRATES: INTERNATIONAL
RIVER VERSUS NATIONAL NEEDS

Disputes over control of river waters are not new in the modern Middle East. Egypt and the Sudan have twice settled their differences over use and development of the Nile amicably, once in 1929 and later in 1959—when the Aswan High Dam was planned. Syria and Jordan reached an agreement in 1953 providing for joint use of the Yarmuk, the chief tributary of the Jordan River; and Iraq and Turkey concluded an agreement in 1946 governing use of the Tigris and Euphrates rivers.

Not all disputes, however, have been settled so peacefully. The decades-long struggle between Jordan and Israel for control of the Jordan River waters is an example of international conflict festering between nations needing the same limited supply, as well as reflecting the wider Arab-Israeli political conflict. Recent development of the Euphrates by Turkey, Syria, and Iraq is injecting a new water dispute into relations between these states, thereby adding fuel to longstanding antagonisms and literally laying the groundwork for future conflict. [2]

In spite of earlier agreements, the development and use of the Euphrates River constitute an issue of increasing concern to Turkey, Syria, and Iraq, the three countries that must share the river. Until the mid-1960s Iraq was the only country to make major use of Euphrates water, but the growing needs of Turkey and Syria and their improved abilities to harness the river's potential during the past 20 years have led to tensions. Iraq fears that if the two upstream nations divert larger and larger amounts of water, the remainder reaching Iraq's southern agricultural regions will be insufficient for necessary irrigation. The population of all three countries has more than doubled since 1940, with Iraq having the highest growth rate (3.3 percent in a population of close to fourteen million, as opposed to Syria's 3.0 percent in eight million and Turkey's 2.6 percent in more than forty million).

Turkey and Syria, understandably, hope to increase their rates of economic growth by developing the river's potential for hydroelectric power and irrigation. And because each is well situated to exploit the river's resources with major dam systems, their long-range development plans include not only current projects but future expansion as well. The view of the Turkish and Syrian governments is that they have a sovereign right to develop their portions of the Euphrates as they see fit, especially since Iraq contributes no water to the Euphrates but extracts large and increasing amounts. (In 1940 Iraq withdrew an estimated 27 percent of Euphrates water flowing through Iraqi territory; by 1969 that amount had increased to 45 percent. Current official figures are not available, but the percentage has increased significantly since 1969.)

The Euphrates has its source in eastern Turkey, then flows southward through Syria, where it is joined by the Khabur, its largest tributary; it then crosses the deserts of Iraq before joining the Tigris and emptying into the Persian Gulf. The river is fed largely from the uplands of northern Turkey, where almost 90 percent of its water originates, with the rest made up in Syria. Iraq contributes no part of the river's waters, but Iraq claims a guaranteed level of water and usage based on continuous historical use, while Syria and Turkey claim priority rights because they control all the river's sources.

Turkey's plans for the river, which it calls the Firat, constitute a 35-year project to produce hydroelectric power and to provide irrigation for expanded agricultural areas. The key to the project is the Keban Dam (first surveyed before World War II, the construction began in 1965 and was completed in 1973), which is designed to control the river's flow and which contains a power plant. Downstream, the river flows through spectacular gorges before running out into foothills near the broad Firat Plains, which have considerable agricultural potential if irrigated. The entire project will add three additional dams—two in the gorges to produce power and one in the lower level for irrigation storage and power—and will construct two canals to divert water to agricultural areas. Once completed, the system will have considerable impact on the volume of the Euphrates River. Even rough estimates are that about 18 percent of the flow at the Keban Dam will be diverted. The Turks claim that the reservoirs will control flow and that even during the driest months the outflow from Turkey will be about one-third the current average and therefore will be more than sufficient for its downstream neighbors' use.

Syria has no worries about the levels of water coming in from Turkey. Inflow from the Khabur into the Euphrates makes up for any deficiencies resulting from Turkish development. The Syrians have large-scale plans for development, with major dam projects on both the Euphrates and the Khabur. The impressive Tabqa Dam on the Euphrates was completed by the Soviet Union after an agreement in 1966 and the Khabur Dam will be equally large. Once both complexes are in operation, the amounts abstracted from the river will be considerable. Also planned is an industrial complex near the Tabqa Dam that will require large amounts of water for cooling and other industrial purposes. Such Syrian use will add industrial effluents to the river, lowering its overall quality as it enters Iraq.

The implications of Turkish and Syrian plans for Iraq are clear if not yet measurable. Iraqi agricultural planning will definitely be affected, since the net result of Turkish and Syrian projects could present serious problems for irrigated agriculture in Iraq. Total flow might be reduced and water quality might be adversely affected by field drainage and evaporation in newly irrigated areas upstream, as well as by industrial pollution from Syrian facilities. Also, Iraqi development planning will have to take into account both the present reductions in water flow—which are not now a problem—and the probability of greater water abstraction or degradation of the system in the future.

Furthermore, any long-range Iraqi planning must consider the droughts that periodically affect the river system, often for years at a time, and must be prepared for serious reductions in available water resources. In an extended drought the upstream dams might permit only a minimal flow of water into Iraq, although this is unlikely because most of the Turkish and Syrian dams are power-generating rather than reservoir dams. The possibility of minimal water reaching Iraq arises not from Turkish or Syrian agricultural and industrial use, but from the limited storage capacity of the projects and the high evaporation rates, which will restrict the ability of upstream governments to maintain even moderate water levels downstream in drought years. Maximum storage capacity of the Turkish and Syrian projects, assuming all are completed, would be only twice the annual flow of the river. Dry spells of even three or four years could produce pressing problems, and a longer drought (such as the one from 1955 to 1962) could raise legitimate concern that Iraq might suffer serious losses because of abnormally low water levels brought about by heavy upstream abstraction for Turkish and Syrian projects.

No one expects that Turkish and Syrian development plans and construction on the Euphrates would soon lead to war or even serious border skirmishes; however, the fear of water being withheld might be more important than whether a serious reduction occurs. The anxiety created in Iraq by the prospect of substantial diversion of what the Iraqis see as their water is precisely the climate likely to produce cycles of accusation and counteraccusation, threat and aggressive response, and the resulting atmosphere that links otherwise unrelated disputes between countries into continuous hostility and suspicion. To know that Middle East countries will not go to war over water is not to say that water disputes will not add further weight to antagonisms already pushing neighbors to war. For example, Iran and Iraq did not go to war over water and the Shatt al-Arab, but that decades-long dispute played a prominent part in the rhetoric each directed against the other and was an element in the emotional climate that produced the war.

The critical factor is that all three countries can rightly claim they need Euphrates waters for their national development. The difficulty, of course, arises from Turkey's (and to some extent, Syria's) claims of usage because the river's sources arise inside its territories, and from Iraq's claims based on long historical use even though none of the river's sources lie inside Iraq. This situation will only worsen because Turkey has considerable land amenable to irrigation from the Euphrates that has not yet even been included in development schemes but that will require further diversion of water from the system if exploited. An important point is that major water consumption from the Euphrates and disputes that will arise from it are likely to increase after 1986 when the Karakaya Dam now under construction, the second of Turkey's proposed three dams, is scheduled for completion. Should the Karakaya Dam and facilities connected to it begin diverting substantial amounts of water at a time when, coincidentally, the natural water levels of the river system are below normal or when there is a prolonged dry spell, the probable Iraqi response could add significant tension to the normally strained relations between Turkey and Syria, on the one hand, and Iraq, on the other.

Events in the spring of 1974 and again in 1975 serve as an example of the potential for confrontations. At that time, Iraq received much lower water levels than normally and claimed that Syria had slowed the flow of water into Iraq as a deliberate maneuver in hostilities between the two governments. Iraq also claimed 70 percent crop damage in the Euphrates Basin and blamed Syria directly for the losses. Syria disclaimed any responsibility, saying that the low water levels originated in Turkey and that Iraqi losses were the result of water diversion in Turkey. But at the same time, the Syrian minister of industry, Mureddin al-Rifai, made clear his government's position on its unequivocal right to development and use of the river in a statement in the Beirut newspaper An-Nahar on May 17, 1975: "The Syrian Euphrates project is Syria's future. The Euphrates region is the new Syria, and Syria will not be able to stand on its own feet and to ensure a stable and prosperous economy in the future unless it is capable of benefiting from its share of Euphrates water. There is no other way." Certainly the Turkish government takes the same view. And although a permanent tripartite commission meets occasionally to discuss development of the river and its resources, no agreement on allocating water or coordinating development projects exists or is likely to in even the long term.

Despite its anxieties, however, Iraq feels confident in its ability to develop the Euphrates in order to minimize the effect of upstream extractions, and to develop the Tigris River for irrigation in the lower Tigris-Euphrates region. In fact, Iraq feels so confident that it recently reached an agreement with Jordan to construct a system for diverting Euphrates waters to northern Jordan in order to aid Jordan in overcoming its increasingly grave water deficit. Such an agreement is, of course, more than just a neighborly arrangement, for it is also part of the larger Arab-Israeli conflict and its consequent struggle over Jordan River waters.

THE JORDAN: WAR, PEACE, AND WATER

The Jordan River provides the most obvious Middle East example of a water dispute that has resisted regional and international settlement for decades. At one time or another, all Jordan Basin states,

as well as the United States and the United Nations, have attempted
to negotiate a common or unified regional plan for the development
and distribution of Jordan waters. Coordinated planning proved unob-
tainable, principally because of wars among the Jordan River neighbors.[3]

Dispute over the resources of the Jordan River system involves
four riparian states: Syria, Lebanon, Jordan, and Israel. Early—
and conflicting—ideas for its development existed before Israel was
created and while the area of all four countries was under the control
of Great Britain or France. Well before serious thought was given
to long-term development needs of the entire basin, the struggle between the British and the French for dominance prevented regional
planning. And after World War II when Syria, Lebanon, Jordan, and
the newly created Israel were struggling with issues of independence
and development, war between Israel and most of its Arab neighbors
had already created the hostile environment that has prevented regional cooperation in Jordan River development for the past 35 years.

Management of the Jordan River system shows clearly the impact of political tensions on the development of limited, yet essential,
water. Although the newly independent states inherited differing views
of proper water development from their French or British mandatory
powers, the disputes over water sharpened into open clashes when the
state of Israel was established and during the subsequent Arab-Israeli
wars of 1948, 1956, 1967, and 1973. The critical turning point was
the 1967 war, which left the West Bank and Golan Heights in Israeli
hands. Previous efforts to negotiate water-use agreements with Jordan, intermittant and frustrating as they had been for all parties including the United States, had at least held the hope that eventually
the antagonists could work out a coordinated, if not unified, scheme
for development and distribution of the region's water. All parties
recognized that water development was essential to industrial and agricultural development, and that coordinated rather than competitive
utilization would produce the greatest benefit. Yet, even before 1967
the riparian states had begun development projects based solely on
individual national needs and, to some extent, on thwarting each other's
use. (By 1967 an agreement had been formulated that was technically
acceptable but still politically impossible.) When the 1967 war ended
so disastrously for the Arab cause, and in particular for Jordan, sustained attempts to reach a settlement on water ended and have not
been resumed. With the West Bank and Jerusalem under Israeli occupation, no Arab neighbor could come to any compromise with Israel
over water, regardless of how necessary and beneficial regional
water-development cooperation might be, and at the same time maintain its self-respect and the regard of the Arab world. The political

price of cooperation was too high, even for the acknowledged benefits of coordinated planning.

To understand how political disputes among the riparian states have distorted current water development of the Jordan River and its tributaries, one must first consider the system as a whole, then examine efforts to establish joint or regional projects, and finally analyze the consequences of their failure.

In the 1950s Syria and Jordan failed to reach acceptable agreements with Israel on development of the Jordan River. After the defeats of 1948 and 1956, Arab states were not inclined to entertain joint projects with Israel, although talks between Jordan and Israel continued sporadically until the early 1960s. Arab suspicions of Israeli long-range plans were confirmed in Arab minds by two circumstances in the years just prior to the 1967 war.

First, the Israelis completed the National Water Carrier in 1964-65. The carrier lies entirely within Israel's pre-1967 boundaries, diverting Jordan water from the northern edge of Lake Tiberias (the Sea of Galilee) and channeling it south through Israel's narrow coastal strip along the Mediterranean to the communities of the Negev Desert. Two points should be made about this water. Because the headwaters of the Jordan lie mostly in Syria and Lebanon, the Arabs thought of the Jordan as carrying "Arab water" to Arab lands. Israel shares only two short reaches of the river as common border. Therefor, when Israel planned and built its National Water Carrier, the Arabs felt the Israelis were taking Arab water for Israeli development. The Israelis, naturally enough, like the Turks in regard to Euphrates development, felt they had the right to develop water resources within their borders and that if their Arab neighbors would not negotiate an agreement to establish cooperative development, Israel could and should proceed independently.

The Arabs, already hostile to Israel and suspicious of its actions, complained that Israel preempted the clean waters of northern Lake Tiberias with the result that the only water Israel returned to the lower Jordan was primarily irrigation runoff. Because Jordan water salinity was already a serious problem, the prospect of diminished and degraded water sources to the West and East banks of Jordan prompted an Arab effort to divert the Jordan even further north than Lake Tiberias. Work began on a system to divert water from Lebanon's Hasbani River through Syria's Golan Heights to the Yarmuk River on the Syrian-Jordanian border. Israeli bombardment of the construction, however, and Israeli successes a short time later in the 1967 war, ended the effort. No further unified Arab attempts was made.

Syria and Jordan, however, had begun a joint project to develop the Yarmuk River and to divert part of its flow into northern Jordanian agricultural areas. Plans originally called for an East Ghor Canal paralleling the east side of the Jordan, and a West Ghor Canal to serve West Bank areas, each continuing almost to the Dead Sea. The canals were necessary to keep the pure waters of the Yarmuk from mixing with the saline waters of the Jordan. The East Ghor Canal has functioned for several years; the West Ghor project was aborted by the 1967 war. Further Syrian-Jordanian plans to develop another dam on the Yarmuk at Mazarin have been halted, primarily because of growing tensions between the two governments in recent years. The Arabs claim that Israel began a struggle for the region's water long before 1967, citing as an example early Zionist plans that included Lebanon's Litani River as being within the geographic boundaries of "Greater Eretz Israel," and saying that the Israelis have always intended to gain control of the whole Jordan River system, including waters from all its tributaries. In negotiations between Israel and Jordan, the Jordanians felt that Israeli development plans were an outgrowth of an early—if later disclaimed—determination to both direct and reap the largest benefit from cooperative development.

The Israelis, on the other hand, saw themselves as surrounded by hostile nations determined, in the worst case, to destroy Israel and, in the best case, to severely limit Israeli territory, access to resources, and future development. In negotiations with Jordan, the Israelis felt the Jordanians wanted to exploit Israeli expertise without granting sufficient benefits to the struggling young country burdened with deserts and limited water.

Given the 15-year-history of Israeli occupation of the West Bank—including the diversion of Jordan River waters deep into Israel without providing water development on the West Bank that benefits equally the native Arab farming villages and the Israeli settlers—the Arabs will certainly be no less suspicious of Israeli intentions should negotiations resume. And Israeli dependence on control of the water resources accessible in the Golan Heights and West Bank territories means that Israel will view any return of control to the Arabs as a direct threat to Israeli development. In the most optimistic view, negotiations would have considerable common ground, in the literal sense, but little common basis for achieving compromise or cooperation.

The Israeli offensive into Lebanon in the summer of 1982 and continued occupation of southern Lebanon in 1983 raise the question of Israeli use of the Litani River. The Israeli government has long-standing feasibility studies for linking the Litani into Israel's National Water Carrier. In general, the plans would call for the Israeli and Lebanese governments, or the Israeli government acting alone in areas under its military control, to cooperate in constructing a tunnel from the point where the Litani descends from its steep gorges to a branch of the Jordan River inside Israeli borders. The Litani flows within two miles of the Israeli border, so a tunnel to divert water as it flows out of the gorges would only have to be one-and-a-half to two-and-a-half miles long in order to channel the water into the upper Jordan, from which it could be moved into the National Water Carrier and distributed throughout the country. Joint projects with Lebanon were not feasible in the late 1960s and 1970s because southern Lebanon became an arena for the struggle among Lebanese, Palestinian refugees, Palestine Liberation Organization (PLO) activists, Syrians, and Israelis. In such a politically charged atmosphere, no Lebanese government could make a wide-ranging development agreement with Israel, regardless of the benefits to its own citizens. Also, no hydro-electric project would have been free of sabotage because the Lebanese government could not provide sufficient security for the construction site or the dam and carrier system once they had been completed.

After the PLO evacuated Beirut and the Israelis were entrenched in southern Lebanon, rumors grew in Beirut that the Israelis had begun to divert Litani waters to Israel. While the rumors were unfounded, the fact that they arose so quickly after Israel established control over the south is testimony to the deep-rooted suspicion among its Arab neighbors that one underlying motive for Israeli military thrusts into Arab territory is the acquisition of extended water sources.[4]

These suspicions are fed by the fact that Israel has continued to develop all water resources to which it has access. Israel's increasing thirst and possible long-range development bear out in Arab minds their suspicions of Israel's expansionist search for water and, at the same time, pose serious problems for the Israeli government. Israel is caught up in what one author calls the hydraulic imperative: the country's increasing need for water, which can only be met by utilizing water available in the Golan Heights and the West Bank, may force Israel to retain control of the occupied territories and, faced with shortages in the near future, to search out yet more new sources of water.[5]

Israeli control of the West Bank provides water for Israel in two ways: directly through water available on the West Bank, and indirectly through Arab development of West Bank water in ways that would limit water entering the aquifer system under the West Bank. It is the replenishing of this aquifer that supplies water along Israel's Mediterranean coastal lands. Implications of the hydraulic imperative, then, are that Israel cannot give up control of the West Bank and the Golan Heights without facing water shortage and curtailment of industrial and agricultural development. Any negotiated withdrawal from the West Bank would have to include provisions for water supplies to Israel.[6]

External political issues aside, the Israeli government will have to confront the domestic issues of water development and distribution. Internal critics question long-standing government support of noneconomic agricultural enterprises that require massive and expensive water supplies. This agricultural support is deeply rooted in Zionist philosophy of return to the land and making the deserts bloom. The social cost of supporting noneconomic or minimally productive agricultural units in an arid country, where most arable land lies in the south while good water sources lie in the north, has proved higher than could have been calculated earlier. Unqualified ideological commitment to agricultural irrigation regardless of social and economic cost has slackened only in the last decade, and the government must soon face allocating water to industrial and urban needs at the expense of agricultural units.[7]

Twice before, Israeli water needs have nearly exceeded supply. In each case, acquisition of new territory has provided new sources. This was true not long after the state was established, it occurred prior to 1967, and it is true once again. The fact that Israeli water demand now consumes all available resources raises fears of water shortage if the West Bank is returned, and this is why access to the Litani River appears important. This fact is also one of the reasons Arab critics were quick to claim that the Israelis were diverting Litani River waters and would remain in southern Lebanon in order to do so. More probably, the case in southern Lebanon is similar to that of 1967, when Israel acquired territory for political and military reasons but soon found that exploiting the newly available resources led to a dependence that would make their return a costly sacrifice.

While Israel has built its strong dependence on Jordan River waters, the Jordanians, in contrast, have made slower progress in utilizing water resources. Jordan in particular feels the loss of control of the Jordan River, the declining quality of lower Jordan waters, and the expense of moving water from the Yarmuk River south to East Bank agricultural areas. Jordan's richest agricultural land, upon which most national food production depends, cannot be adequately developed to keep pace with population growth without extensive and costly irrigation. The lower Jordan is now so saline, from both Israeli and Jordanian irrigation, that the East Ghor Canal had to be constructed to carry Yarmuk River waters south rather than mix them with the saline lower Jordan.

Jordan has gone from having a healthy water surplus in 1977 to a rapidly increasing deficit in 1983, a deficit that will severely limit further development and will lead to a decline in living standards un-

less it is made up from outside water sources. Thus, the Iraqi-
Jordanian agreement to divert Euphrates waters to northern Jordan
is of critical importance to Jordan's future and will no doubt affect
the Jordanian government's flexibility on political issues upon which
Jordan and Iraq may disagree. This is an example of how the Arab-
Israeli conflict has prevented regional water cooperation that could
have averted or forestalled Jordan's water crisis, and how, consequently, in its search for water Jordan has had to turn to a hard-line
neighbor for help. This has resulted in a practical alliance that will
make it more difficult for Jordan to join peace efforts.

The Lebanese have not been able to exploit the Litani or Hasbani rivers because of the increasing violence in southern Lebanon
after 1970 and the destruction from the civil war that broke out in
1975. One major project the Lebanese government will no doubt wish
to initiate once rebuilding of basic infrastructure is under way, is
development of the Litani both for irrigation and for hydroelectric
power. Whether the Lebanese will undertake such development by
using international aid or by working out a joint development scheme
with Israel, the effort will be fraught with political difficulties.

Prospects for regional cooperation in Jordan River development
are tied to the settlement of the Israeli-Palestinian-Arab struggle.
Without a resolution that leaves the parties open to joint and regional
efforts, exploitation of the Jordan River system will continue to be
narrowly nationalistic, competitive, and limited. As a result, the
Arab riparian states, faced with rapidly rising populations without increased agricultural production, will be unable to develop their chief
water sources as fully or as efficiently as would be the case if regional
cooperation were possible. Israel, in contrast, will find that its successful agricultural and industrial development will make it increasingly vulnerable to water shortages, forcing Israeli society to confront the social costs of supporting noneconomic agriculture for
deeply held ideological reasons, and at the same time making any exchange of territory in future peace negotiations hydraulically expensive. The potential for conflict over water or for conflicts including
water issues increases constantly as each society's need for water
rises without an ability to make more available. And while war over
Jordan waters is improbable, water-system sabotage is certainly
not out of the question, and negotiations with water as a critical element are likely in the next decade.

WATER CONFLICT IN THE MIDDLE EAST CONTEXT

The examples of the Euphrates and Jordan rivers demonstrate
the problems arising from water management and development in the

Middle East and their potential for international conflict. If nothing else, examining water issues reconfirms—if anyone doubts—that Middle East issues on every level are extremely complex and that no monolithic answer is acceptable. A political solution to the Palestinian conflict will improve prospects for the region, but it would be only a step toward solving the serious problems of growth and development faced by all Middle East states. Real issues divide these states other than the squabbles between Ba'athist Syria and Ba'athist Iraq, the struggle between revolutionary Iran and its neighbors, or the conflict between the Arabs and Israelis. The existence of these political and ethnic conflicts should not blind us to the region's fundamental needs, nor should it lead us to think that solving the major political disputes alone will solve the region's problems.

It is no exaggeration to say that the future of these societies depends on their ability to conserve, harness, and manage the region's water. And unlike oil, water is a shared resource. When water problems become acute, international discussions must take place in the tense and often hostile atmosphere of crisis, made worse by the fact that once the crisis occurs, options for limiting the damage or cooperatively solving the problem have been substantially limited by separate, competitive development. Water has already proved to be an important element of diplomacy and regional relations and will undoubtedly assume a larger and more divisive role in the future. While specialists in water management may recognize the need for regional water planning, U.S. government policy makers do not consider the fundamental nature of such unified management to the agricultural and industrial development of Middle East countries.

Older stereotypes of the Middle East, with their deserts and camels, were as faulty and simplistic as stereotypes always are—but at least we could not miss the importance of water to the region regardless of how little else we understood. Our newer stereotypes, in contrast, give us oil-rich princes in Rolls Royce limousines and terrorists with machine guns and hostages. Do we forget the fine and shifting line that has always existed between the desert land and the sown land in the Middle East? Water determines the difference, which Middle East peoples remember even if we do not.

NOTES

1. For a discussion of the role of technology in development and, in particular, the ways in which science and technology affect developing societies, see Graham Jones, The Role of Science and Technology in Developing Countries (London: Oxford University Press,

1971). Jones concludes that management is probably the most important factor, especially the need to apply improved management to watersheds and to safeguard water supplies from pollution. For a varied look at water issues in developing countries, see World Health Organization, "Water, Source and Sustenance of Life," Impact of Science on Society 26 (1974): 237-38; United Nations Water Conference Secretariat, "Assessment of the World Water Situation," EKISTICS 43 (1977): 5-8; E. W. Coward, Jr., "Indigenous Organization, Bureaucracy and Development: The Case of Irrigation," Journal of Development Studies 13 (1976): 92-105; D. Bromley, "Water Reform and Economic Development," Economic Development and Cultural Change 28 (1980): 365-87; and Asit K. Biswas, "Water for the Third World," Foreign Affairs 60 (1981): 148-66.

2. For a brief introduction to the international ramifications of Euphrates River development, see Peter Beaumont, "The Euphrates River—An International Problem of Resource Development," Environmental Conservation 5 (1978): 35-44; and Zohurul Bari, "Syrian-Iraqi Dispute over the Euphrates Waters," International Studies 16 (1977): 227-44. Beaumont has also written about other water issues affecting the Middle East.

3. The Jordan River dispute as a whole has been examined extensively. For an introduction to the dispute, see Georgiana Stevens, Jordan River Partition (Stanford, Calif.: Stanford University Press, Hoover Institution on War, Revolution and Peace, 1965); Samir N. Saliba, The Jordan River Dispute (The Hague: Martinus Nijhoff, 1968); and C. G. Smith, "The Disputed Waters of the Jordan," Institute of British Geographers, Transactions, no. 40 (December 1966), pp. 111-28.

4. Private conversations. The Lebanese government took the rumors seriously enough to send a military commander to the southern Litani area to learn whether the Israelis were undertaking construction on the river.

5. Thomas R. Stauffer, "The Price of Peace: The Spoils of War," American-Arab Affairs 1 (1982): 43-54.

6. For a discussion of the issue of Israeli control of water resources on the West Bank and its political implications, see Stauffer, "Price of Peace"; and John Stebbings, "The Creation of a Palestinian Arab State as Part of a Middle East Settlement," International Relations 6 (1979): 635-44.

7. For an overview of the domestic context of Israeli water policy, see Itzak Galnoor, "Water Policymaking in Israel," Policy Analysis 3 (1978): 339-67.

11

DEVELOPMENT DIPLOMACY

EDWARD E. AZAR

Relations between the United States and Third World countries
are directly linked with issues of U.S. development assistance. One
major component of each Third World country's relationship with the
United States is the solicitation—or rejection—of aid monies. The
United States and the Soviet Union compete to furnish aid where they
see opportunities to influence local governments in directions that
support their own ideological and international positions, or to pre-
empt the acceptance of aid from the other. The tug-of-war over aid
recipients, matched by Third World maneuvering to obtain the aid,
is an economic and political minuet so familiar that we take it for
granted. Seldom any longer do U.S. political leaders raise the cry
to cut off all foreign aid; disputes about aid rage over amounts to be
given and who should receive them.

A large proportion of U.S. aid is for development. Consequently, the diplomacy of U.S. development aid now dominates many of the
ways both the United States and Third World countries view their relationships. This chapter describes the type of relations the United
States should pursue in dealing with developing countries, especially
those in the Near East now experiencing wrenching social conflict,
and provides a conceptual base for a process I call development diplomacy.

Three important points bring into focus the issues of development diplomacy. First, most Third World countries experience great

instability and internal violence. According to Conflict and Peace
Data Bank records at the University of Maryland, some 90 percent
of the world's total violence since the end of World War II has occurred in the Third World. Second, the nature and sources of this
violence are complex. Most violence is based on group conflict over
issues of ethnic, cultural, linguistic, and/or religious acceptance
and integration into the society at large. Virtually no Third World
country is homogeneous, and some are riven by the struggle between
competing religions, ethnic groups, and linguistic groups. This
struggle and the violence accompanying it are protracted and appear
to absorb the energies of most people in these societies. At times
these group conflicts (which some analysts call identity-based conflicts) are confined to one geographic region or to a single nation,
but often they spread across borders and regions. Their most important aspect is that they continually produce and reproduce instability, enlarging the circle of violence and raising the already high
risk to regional or world peace. And, of course, each conflict becomes an arena for superpower competition, adding to the violence
and anxiety over peace.

Third, conflict resolution in the international system has tended
to be formalistic and legalistic, with none of the flexibility necessary
to successfully confront the international ramifications of Third World
instability and upheaval. Traditional diplomacy has tended to focus
on ending the violent incidents and, more optimistically, on lowering
the incidence of violence, but it relies on documentary or formal approaches to do so. While effective in some instances, these methods
have not usually been successful. Because they are based on the
same approach, UN, bilateral, and multinational efforts at conflict
resolution in the traditional sense have also been ineffective.

Traditional diplomacy has not been able to address group-based
or identity-based conflicts in a manner commensurate with the problem. Rather, the combination of a traditional approach with a more
comprehensive attack on the interrelated social and economic problems in the Third World, with a clear picture of the desired social
change for these areas, will be the best ensurance of success. Hence,
I propose the concept of development diplomacy.

THE EXTENT AND NATURE OF
CONFLICT IN THE THIRD WORLD

There are several ways of describing, discovering, and ex-
plaining sources of conflict in the Third World as a whole and in the
Near East in particular. But underlying all descriptions are three

common points. First, conflict situations caused by inequalities
built into the social systems of the countries concerned tend to be
protracted. Second, they divert the world's time and resources, as
well as those of the unstable country itself, and reduce the ability
and will of capable or interested actors to "solve" them. And, finally,
these conflicts tend to defy the unilateral or multilateral management
skills applied to them.

Social conflicts based on inequalities between groups within a
society are protracted, hostile interactions extending over generations and centuries, with sporadic outbreaks of open warfare that
fluctuate in frequency and intensity. This struggle between groups is
also reflected within each individual member of society, since the individual must belong to both a group and to the society as a whole.
Such hostile conflict sometimes involves different groups within one
nation-state or groups in neighboring nation-states where deep-seated
racial, ethnic, and religious hatreds generate domestic and international hostilities or intensify existing differences. Because such long-
term social conflicts are rooted in intrinsic characteristics of the
peoples involved—ethnic, linguistic, racial, and religious—the actual
distribution of power and resources or the perceived distribution patterns play a crucial role in the hostilities. Protracted social conflicts differ from other types of conflict in that they focus on group
identity and personal identity in relation to the power and privileges
associated with each group. Especially in the Third World, these
conflicts are insidious and pervasive, tending to pose several inter-
locking crises simultaneously, all of which are tied to past and present injustices and inequities and all of which affect present leadership.

Social systems skewed economically, politically, militarily,
or socially in favor of one group over others—and this description fits
virtually all Third World countries—seem to invite protracted social
conflicts. Since the conflicts feed on domestic hatred and inequalities,
and since the society's economic and social structures reinforce the
inequalities and distinctions that produce the hatred in the first place,
the cycle of violence is extremely difficult to break. Relations with
outsiders usually intensify these internal cycles of hatred and violence
because international economic, political, informational, and technological structures always connect with internal groups in terms of
their respective power and status. In other words, those groups with
greater wealth, power, and status are usually the ones that gain the
most from contacts with the outside. (In the few cases in which the
reverse is true, when contact with outsiders dramatically alters the
relative status of groups in a society, intergroup hatred and violence
still result.) For members of these societies, the conflicts are full-
time crises that exhaust the limited human and physical resources
available to ameliorate or resolve them.

The causes of inequality are not simply levels of wealth or economic productivity. Rather, the distribution of rewards in a society, whether status, wealth, or access to power, is a function of the distribution of power—that is, the organizational structures and differential control that various groups have over production. Such a definition refers to economic power only, and power derived from control of economic assets and organization of production must be differentiated from power relations based on political power.

Because economic power relations stem from positions in economic production and its social organization, some analysts have identified power positions based on economics with power positions based on political control. This view is rather mechanistic in that it supposes a direct correspondence between positions in the two spheres, and is also "economistic" in that it considers that all relations in a society, even those involving ideology, sociology, and politics, are essentially permutations of economic relations. It is true that varying degrees of economic power held by different groups in a society will necessarily lead to certain economic and social inequalities between the groups, but these "structural inequalities"—built into the society's structure—grow out of the complex interplay of economic and political power positions of the different groups. No simple correlation between economic power and political power adequately delineates the political and economic power relations between groups.

THE MIDDLE EAST CONTEXT AND
THE CHALLENGE OF DEVELOPMENT

Because of its oil, geopolitics, and market, the strategic significance of the Middle East has dominated U.S. thinking on the region, especially in relation to the Arab-Israeli conflict. Soviet and U.S. involvement in the Middle East and superpower interactions elsewhere in the world have made a serious impact on relations among Arabs and between the Arabs and Israelis. During the intense superpower cold-war rivalry in the 1950s and early 1960s, the Arabs split into opposing camps, siding with one or the other power, and intra-Arab suspicion and hostilities intensified. The propaganda war between North Atlantic Treaty Organization (NATO) and Warsaw Pact states heightened the virulence of intra-Arab and Arab-Israeli verbal warfare. Over a 30-year period, the superpowers supplied their respective Middle East clients with sophisticated arms and with moral and political support. Such support has at times become imbalanced and thereby has precipitated war within the Middle East. Recent U.S.

actions have helped to narrow Egyptian-Israeli differences, but Soviet-U.S. competition in the Persian Gulf, the Red Sea, the Horn of Africa, and elsewhere in the Third World will inevitably have repercussions in the Arab-Israeli setting and therefore will work to maintain the conflict.

Both levels of the Arab-Israeli conflict—the ethnic and the interstate or strategic—cannot be fully understood without linking them to issues of national and regional development. In order to make such a linkage, the process of development must be defined as the process by which a community organizes itself in coping with change in its physical or social environment. In this case, organization refers to the structure of connections (what could be called interdependencies) between the economic, political, technological, and value systems that, in a broad sense, constitute the community. The purpose of any national or regional development plan, therefore, must be to reorganize this structure so the community's capacity to mediate between the needs of the human population and the potential of its physical environment increases. However, contemporary development thought is unable to meet this requirement because, in its desire to discover a simpler or more elegant solution, it tends to ignore these complex interdependencies, which the community has developed over generations to enable its members to best use its resources. Instead, development thought tends to produce policy recommendations that are appropriate in terms of theory but that come to grief when implemented in a given society.

I am sympathetic to the fact that growth in the productive sector, especially in nations with rapidly increasing populations, is a necessity if improvement in the physical quality of life is not to be sacrificed, or in some cases if already low standards are not to fall even lower under population pressure. However, the assumption that such growth has a uniform effect on all societies is clearly false. I would argue that a successful policy of fostering growth in productive capacity must be preceded by a careful structural analysis of society that must include an in-depth study of specific social relations. Furthermore, the concepts around which to organize such an analysis are crucial because they determine how the structure is exposed for examination.

I suggest that the core goal of any meaningful development plan must be to reduce inequality. Not only does growth of the economic sector without reduction of inequality seem morally lacking, but I would argue that it will also be doomed to failure as the economic system becomes hyperdeveloped and is no longer organically related to the rest of the social organization. Such disconnection between economic and social systems produces social breakdown, with the first casualty being the development plan and most of its accomplishments.

The concept of "structural victimization," the idea that in each society the social system builds inequalities into its structure and thereby creates victims of its social structure, will be helpful in clarifying the linkage between development and social conflict in general, and specifically in the case of the Arab-Israeli conflict. I suggest that to increase victimization by producing new inequalities or by extending existing ones to critical levels is likely to produce violence, making general violence more likely and rendering peace more unstable, although targets of the violence will be difficult to predict.

The sources of victimization structured into the Middle East social system are many and varied. The most obvious set of structures that both impede development and increase victimization have been created by the Arab-Israeli conflict itself. In addition to the obvious fact that an individual's personal health and safety are in constant jeopardy, the conflict leads each government to interfere more and more in the affairs of its citizens in the interest of national security, and the state is forced to expend a larger and larger proportion of its attention and resources on the conflict rather than on internal problems. The overwhelming fact of the conflict, its very existence, has obscured the necessity to seek the conflict's roots and to recognize how the conflict relates to the rest of the social structure, while simultaneously reducing the resources available for such a task. Thus, alternatives to war are not considered. Not surprisingly, very little has been done about meaningful development, and the more acute problems of underdevelopment have been tackled only in situations in which the cumulative effects of economic decay have already placed the regime's stability in jeopardy.

In much the same way as conflict theory has tended to concentrate on violence as an overt manifestation of conflict, most development theory tends to focus on some indicator of growth, usually in the economic sector. In focusing on economic growth as the goal, even if reduction of gross inequality is considered to be an important means to the goal, we are likely to be misled as a reduction in victimization or inequality is traded off against, say, political order in the interest of economic growth. Because no sustained economic growth can occur unless it is accompanied by reorganization of the rest of the social system with which the economy is interdependent, development policies focusing solely on economic development are doomed to fail. Thus, we need to focus on interdependencies in social structure when designing development plans.

This argument has a certain intuitive appeal. Why, then, are economic development models still the major tool for development planning and research? How can planners assume that economic development naturally leads, at the least, to improved physical quality of life and reduction in the built-in inequalities I have called structural victimization? Again, as with conflict theory, economic models seem to match the historical experience of the developed Western nations very nicely. I would argue, as above, that this is largely because these theories are little more than generalizations or formalizations of the historical experience of the nations in which they were invented, and as such, are of limited usefulness in studying radically different social and physical environments. A second, less charitable explanation is that economic development models not only describe the Western development experience well, but also are fundamentally simple, clear, and logical, thus sparing the analyst the difficult and frustrating work of exposing the complex connections and interdependencies in the social organization and historical development of non-Western societies.

These economic models are also comforting to political elites in the states seeking development because the models hold the hope of economic growth and general improvement in the physical quality of life without requiring large-scale social reorganization that is so destabilizing. That hope, however, is a mirage. As a result of the interdependencies among all sectors of the social structure, massive change cannot occur in any single part of society without a ripple of adjustments throughout the entire structure. The nature of these adjustments is conditioned by the specific structure of the social organization as bounded by its physical and social environment. Thus, simple assumptions about the relationship between economic development and general improvement in quality of life are misleading.

Examination of data on the physical quality of life and population trends in the Middle East, as reflected in UN studies and others, confirms the probability of continuing increases in structural inequalities and victimization. Even if present-day peace initiatives succeed, serious social problems and economic shortages will persist, for the basic sources of social inequalities in Middle East societies lie not in the Arab-Israeli conflict, but in the social systems of the individual societies. Even if the region were at peace, these inequalities would produce formidable economic and social problems, exacerbated by the prospect of shortages. While it is commonplace to discuss shortages that affect us all, in the Middle East shortage is already a terrifying reality.

Furthermore, the very fact of shortage is in itself conducive to structural inequality or victimization, for given the kinds of social, political, and economic structures existing in the Middle East, victimization quickly proceeds from probability to fact. The structures producing the inequality are at times themselves relatively stable; the crucial parameter is rapid population growth.

At its least, rapid population growth in the less-developed countries of the Middle East increases the absolute number of poor people. And by increasing the population's dependency ratio—that is, the ratio between, on the one hand, those aged 14 and under and those over 65, and on the other hand, those in the presumably more productive age bracket of 15 to 64—the relative number of poor people is increased. With increases in both the absolute and relative numbers of poor people, structural victimization is by definition increased. Therefore, population growth in the region makes it inescapable that without significant social change (social reorganization to reduce inequalities at their root), structural victimization is almost certain to increase, and with it the violence that inevitably accompanies such sustained inequality.

Once one concludes that a substantial amount of inequality in the world is structured by social systems and that there is no real hope of reducing social violence unless one succeeds in alleviating aspects of the systems producing the inequality and the violence, one faces the arduous task of pursuing this goal of alleviation. Relying on traditional solutions—concentrating on economic growth, for example—leads to reinforcing some of the vested interests in the status quo that actually cause much of the very problem in need of elimination. By choosing an innovative approach, one often runs up against ineffectuality, contradiction, moral dilemmas, and forces wishing to keep things just as they are.

Attempts to wipe out structural inequality, whether actual or potential, direct or indirect, can succeed only if they are unremitting. Difficulties and setbacks are to be expected, for counterintuitive, inertia-bound, and notoriously ungovernable social systems do not lend themselves to specific predictions, and therefore they defy prescription. In the interests of social change and peace, we must be persistent and willing to risk some trial and error as we plan for the future.

OPTIONS FOR U.S. FOREIGN POLICY IN THE 1980s

The choice of options in the Middle East has never been easy for the United States. Future options may turn out to be profitable, but they require tough and creative decisions. It is my contention that the United States faces a decisive period in which creative approaches must be employed to deal with Middle East regional and international politics.

Past interactions with the region have tended to be fragmented, apparently disconnected, and often contradictory, thereby creating ample distrust and even dislike of the United States and its representatives in some parts of the region. However, there is also a deep reservoir of admiration and respect for the United States and the West. The United States should now capitalize on the positive and should rebuild comprehensive regional linkages for tackling the problems of peace and development. The Middle East economic environment is ripe for U.S. involvement, but this involvement must be mutually beneficial. How?

Peace and development in a comprehensive regional plan will accomplish goals long cherished by the United States. An economically developed Middle East will provide benefits for the United States, and a regionally integrated Middle East will both enhance U.S. exports to the region and help U.S. business throughout the area. A stable and developed Middle East will enhance the political fortunes and, by extension, the security objectives of the West.

It may be argued that short-term policies are attractive and profitable, and that the United States could benefit more by isolating the oil-rich Arabs from the capital-hungry Arabs. Or, believing it to be a good short-term strategy, the United States could absorb as much as possible of the region's surpluses during the coming decade. Or, furthermore, it could be argued that concluding bilateral political, military, and economic agreements is easy and appears to work.

Nothing is more inaccurate than this approach. If the United States pursues its present course, the Middle East will be even more impoverished and violent in the next 15 years than it is now. As a consequence, U.S. exports to the area will fall to negligible levels. If Arab-Israeli wars continue, instability will increase throughout the region, as it already has steadily done during the past 30 years. Inter-Arab wars will grow in scope and number. Bilateral or multilateral security arrangements with a few regimes, without dealing with matters of domestic and regional stability and peace, will not work in the long run. This security approach has not worked in the past—all U.S. security initiatives of the 1950s failed—and I see no reason for it to work in the 1980s. By pursuing narrow and seemingly disconnected policies in the Middle East, the United States is likely to exhaust its diplomatic and political base.

However, by pursuing a comprehensive regional policy of peace and development, much as it did in Western Europe after World War II, the United States would gain the Middle East nations as allies in the same way that Europe and the United States are allies, not always in agreement but sharing common values and commitments. If the United States, with its own financial resources and those of the Middle East, advocates and supports a program of creative development, it will protect its own interests in that vital part of the world and will aid the region's peoples.

Regarding the military aspect, if the United States takes a long-term perspective and devises ways of working with diverse types of regimes, then the defense capability of the United States and the West will be increased. On the question of Arab-Israeli conflict, if the United States can help solve the Palestinian-Israeli conflict, it will have neutralized the Palestinian and Arab Left. Neither President Carter's Camp David approach nor President Reagan's Jordanian option approach of August 1982 addresses the twin sides of the Middle East dilemma—namely, that peace and development must go together. Diplomatic and security arrangements that do not recognize and take into account the structural characteristics of individual Middle East societies, and that do not work to alleviate inequalities resulting from them, will not serve the long-term interests of a stable Middle East.

Addressing these issues are instrumental aspects of a comprehensive regional policy that champions a development diplomacy. Retrenchment, for the United States, is neither possible nor desirable, and an elective bilateral involvement contains elements of narrowness and ultimate danger. Only a comprehensive regional policy promoting development and peace is in the best interests of the United States.

The United States must pursue a grand design that recognizes diversity of modes of change, supports democratic institutions, provides active assistance in basic needs, and designs internationally accommodative policies. This is in keeping with properties of the present world system, because it recognizes that the logic of rivalry between the superpowers in a bipolar system, and the apparent reduction of their preoccupation to spheres of influence and strategic considerations, can only generate a protracted threat and disastrous consequences.

The strategic analyst may point out that this approach would deprive the United States of the support of many regimes around the world in return for hypothetical future support or much less dependable opposition. Others may suggest that the developmental approach for U.S. diplomacy disregards domestic U.S. interest groups favoring policies abroad that may contradict the logic of the comprehensive developmental approach. Additionally, it might be argued that such an approach would be costly if the United States were to shoulder the responsibility of providing sufficient aid and other support to promote Third World development.

These objections may prove to be justified in the short run. However, no one argues that the United States must shoulder all the responsibility. Rather, the United States should design its own comprehensive developmental approach and then assess what is involved and who is to be involved and in what ways. This is necessary because

political and social change will be detrimental to U.S. interests if
the United States appears to lack a thorough plan for dealing creatively
with emerging world events. Policies toward underdeveloped countries that directly or indirectly support internal structural inequality,
regional insecurity, and continued underdevelopment will invite rejection and opposition to the United States. Only tolerance of different
regimes and regime changes, matched with support for the reduction
of inequality, insecurity, and instability, will win the United States
its most valuable strategic asset—namely, the support of the region's
populations.

U.S.-LEBANESE RELATIONS: A GOOD
PROSPECT FOR DEVELOPMENT DIPLOMACY

Lebanon is typical of many of the developing nations described
earlier in this chapter because it has been embroiled in protracted
social conflict. Facing internal social and economic problems and
subjected to external intervention and an influx of foreign population,
Lebanon has paid a high cost in human, material, and psychological
terms. The country's roads, buildings, and infrastructure have been
destroyed or seriously eroded, and at present, Lebanon remains occupied militarily and politically.

Recent events in the Middle East have altered the region's political map. A new stability is gradually being built, with U.S. support,
for Lebanese independence and sovereignty, and in addition, the
Lebanese themselves seem to have acquired a new determination to
rid themselves of foreign forces and to rebuild their state and their
economy. But no amount of optimism will provide answers to the following questions:

What is involved in the transition from war to peace in Lebanon?
What psychological, institutional, or physical changes are required? Are these short-term or long-term changes?
What role can the United States play in this new setting, and
how might development diplomacy be applied to the Lebanese case?

We cannot know the answers yet, but the following ideas might
provide partial answers. The United States can be a positive force
in healing Lebanon's wounds and in propelling the country onto the
road to recovery from war, for U.S. support has a great impact on
Lebanon's internal and regional situation. Presently, a national consensus exists in Lebanon that the United States is Lebanon's best possible ally, and the United States is considered to be capable of deliv-

ering political security and economic support to Lebanon for many years to come. At the same time, Lebanon can provide numerous opportunities for advancing U.S. interests in the region. In this sense, Lebanon can become part of the solution rather than part of the problem.

Any U.S. support for internal Lebanese stability and for regional peace will be a great asset to U.S. diplomacy interests. Secure domestic and regional environments without prejudice toward one group or state over others would be an essential component of active U.S. participation in regional affairs. In concrete terms, U.S. participation in the multinational force, in the tripartite negotiations for withdrawal of foreign forces from Lebanon, in the rebuilding of the Lebanese army and security institutions, in the expansion of international support for internal Lebanese coexistence, and in the maintenance of good external relations in the region, will all boost U.S. credibility and centrality in the region. Should the United States attempt to engage in unique or limited bilateral security arrangements that threaten any group or state, negative consequences for both Lebanon and the United States will result.

The U.S. role in Lebanon's physical security is only one aspect of the development diplomacy explained above; the other components are economic well-being and political stability. All these elements are essential and must be woven together. Without the physical security and stability of Lebanon and the region, it will be hard to make headway on other fronts. No effective development diplomacy can succeed in Lebanon, Jordan, Syria, or elsewhere in the Middle East if domestic stability and regional peace are not addressed.

In the economic sphere, the United States can help in two ways. First, it can provide psychological and moral support for aid and investment in Lebanon's future, and second, it can take steps to increase both the investment pool and the private-sector support for Lebanon's infrastructure.

The United States has already taken steps to provide a leadership role for the development of Lebanon's economy, but that is a long-term project. At present, domestic economic troubles hamper U.S. mobility in foreign investment, as do some aspects of Organization of Petroleum Exporting Countries policies and activities. Political boredom and long delays in making progress in Lebanon appeal to those who want the United States to step aside and do nothing in development diplomacy. All these factors should influence the United States to take bolder steps in assisting Lebanon as fully as necessary. While it is hard at this point to judge future U.S. steps in Lebanon, it appears that development support is headed in the right direction.

INDEX

ABOUT THE EDITORS AND CONTRIBUTORS

JOYCE R. STARR, Editor of this volume, is Overseas Representative in the Middle East for the Center for Strategic and International Studies (CSIS). She is also Middle East Editor of the CSIS Washington Quarterly. In 1982–83 Dr. Starr served as Director of the Secretariat of the U.S. Business Commission on the Reconstruction of Lebanon, a U.S. government initiative. Prior to joining CSIS, she was associate special assistant in the White House during the Carter administration, where she participated in the Interagency Task Force on the Economic Implications of a Middle East Peace Settlement. Earlier Dr. Starr served with a number of U.S. commissions and national organizations, including the U.S. Privacy Protection Commission and the National Endowment for the Humanities. She received an undergraduate degree from the University of Michigan and an M.A. and Ph.D. from Northwestern University-Chicago.

ADDEANE S. CAELLEIGH, Associate Editor of this volume, is a Research Associate at the Center for Strategic and International Studies, where she is specializing in the Middle East. A cultural geographer and historian, she has taught at the college and university levels and written on the Middle East. Before joining CSIS, Ms. Caelleigh was a Researcher at the University of Sydney, where she coauthored Britain's Elusive Empire in the Middle East, 1914–21 (1981). She holds an M.A. from the University of West Florida and has completed several years of doctoral study and research at the University of Texas-Austin.

EDWARD AZAR is Director of the Center for International Development at the University of Maryland. Previously, he was Director of Studies of Conflict and Peace at the University of North Carolina-Chapel Hill, after serving on the faculties of Michigan State University and the Massachusetts Institute of Technology.

FRED GOTTHEIL is Professor of Economics at the University of Illinois and former Chairman of the Department of Economics. He has written numerous articles and books on economics and is currently the President of Professors for Peace in the Middle East.

FAWZI HABIB is Senior Adviser for the International Finance Corporation in Washington, D.C., where he has served for over fifteen years. Previously, he was Financial Adviser to the President of Panama, Senior Economist for the International Bank for Reconstruction and Development, and Professor of Economics at Florida State University.

ZEEV HIRSCH is Mel and Sheila Jaffee Professor of International Trade at the Leon Racanati Graduate School of Business Administration, Tel Aviv University, and is former Dean of its School of Business. He is the author of Location of Industry and International Competitiveness (1967), The Export Performance of Six Manufacturing Industries: A Comparative Study of Denmark, Holland and Israel (1971), and Rich Man's, Poor Man's and Everyman's Goods (1977) and coauthor of Economics of Peacemaking—Focus on the Middle East (1983).

SHIREEN T. HUNTER is a Political and Economic Consultant, specializing in the Middle East, for Malmgren, Inc., of Washington, D.C. She served with the Foreign Service of Iran in positions of increasing responsibility in Iran, Europe, and the United States, including First Secretary and then Counselor at the Permanent Mission of Iran to the Office of the United Nations in Geneva.

MAX KOHNSTAMM is President of the European Community Institute for University Studies and former President, until 1981, of the European University Institute of Florence. He was directly involved in the work that led to the creation of the European Economic Community, including service with the High Authority of the European Coal and Steel Community and with the Action Committee for the United States of Europe.

JEROME I. LEVINSON is General-Counsel for the Inter-American Development Bank, the oldest and largest regional development bank, and also a lecturer at the Johns Hopkins University School of Advanced International Studies. Previously, he served as Counsel to the U.S. Senate Foreign Relations Subcommittee on Multinational Corporations, as Senior American Policy Adviser to the President of the Inter-American Development Bank, and as Assistant Director of an AID mission to Brazil.

NADEEM G. MAASRY is a Financial Adviser in Washington, D.C., offering services to overseas clients investing in the United States. Until 1982 he was Vice-president of Financial General Bankshares, a multibank holding company, after previously serving as Vice-president of the International Bank of Washington.

ABDUL R. A. MEGUID, a prominent Egyptian leader, served as Deputy Prime Minister of Egypt for Economic and Financial Affairs as well as the Minister of Economy, Finance and Planning under the late Anwar Sadat and, for five months, under President Mubarak.

ROBERT R. NATHAN is an internationally known economist and Chairman of Robert R. Nathan Associates, Inc. He previously served in major positions in the U.S. government, including Deputy Director of the Office of War Mobilization and Reconversion, Chairman of the War Production Board Planning Committee, Chief of the Requirements Division of the Defense Advisory Commission and Office of Production Management, and Chief of the National Income Division of the U.S. Department of Commerce.